CATCH
and other stories

CRAZY
HORSE
PRESS

www.crazyhorsepress.com

i

CRAZY
HORSE
PRESS

© S. Bowkett 1988
A modified version of this book
was first published by Victor Gollancz 1988
and by Piper Books 1990.
This edition: Crazy Horse Press 2000
ISBN 1 871870 13 5

Printed by T. Snape & Co Ltd., Boltons Court, Preston PR1 3TY. Tel: 01772 254553 Fax: 01772 204697

Other Titles by Steve Bowkett

- *Spellbinder (teen fantasy)* - Gollancz 1985/Tellerup 1986/Pan 1988.
- *The Copy Cat Plan* - Blackwell 1986.
- *Gameplayers (teen fantasy)* - Gollancz 1986/Pan 1988.
- *Dualists (teen fantasy)* - Gollancz 1987/Pan 1989/Praha 1993.
- *Catch & Other Stories (teen genre)* - Gollancz 1988/Pan 1990.
- *Frontiersville High (teen SF)* - Gollanez 1990.
- *The Community (adult horror)* - Pan 1993.
- *The Bidden (adult horror)* - Pan 1994.
- *A Rare Breed (adult horror)* - Pan 1996
- *Panic Station (teen horror)* - Henderson 1996/Gallimard 1996.
- *Dinosaur Day (young fantasy)* - Heinemann Banana Book 1996.
- *For The Moon There Is The Cloud (tales in the Zen tradition)* - Collins, Pathways Reading Scheme, 1996.
- *The World's Smallest Werewolf* - Macdonald, Shivery Storybooks 1996.
- *Meditations For Busy People (How to Stop Worrying & Stay Calm)* - HarperCollins 1996 (USA 1996 as *A Little Book Of Joy*).
- *Dreamcastle (pre-teen SF)*, Orion Children's Books 1997/Mondadori, Italy '97 (also Germany, Portugal, Norway, France and China).
- *Dino Discoveries (non fiction 7+)* - Henderson FunFax Dinosaur File, 1997.
- *Imagine That! A Handbook Of Creative Learning Activities for the Classroom*, Network Educational Press, 1997.
- *Another Girl, Another Planet (adult SF, with Martin Day)* - Virgin New Adventures, 1998.
- *Roy Kane - TV Detective* - A&C Black's Graffix series, 1998, p/b '99.
- *Self-Intelligence* - A Handbook for Developing Confidence, Self Esteem & Interpersonal Skills, Network Educational Press, 1999.
- *Dreamcatcher* - for Orion's Dreamtime teen fantasy/horror series, Spring 2000.
  (Steve is also Consultant Editor for this series).
- *Horror at Halloween/Eleanor* - a Horror novella which is one segment of a 'mosaic novel', Pumpkin Books, Spring 2000.

Short Stories

- *Graveyard Orbit* - Harper-Collins SF Tape, 1993.
- *Barry* - Fantastic Space Stories, 1993/Braille & Talking Books for the Blind, '97.
- *...And Eternity In An Hour* - Decalog 3, (Dr Who), Virgin, '96.
- *Emily Bites* - Creepy Stories - Doubleday, '96.
- *Intelligent Life Elsewhere* - Space Stories, Robinson, 1996/Random House Book of Science Fiction Stories, 1997.
- *The Final Program* - Orion 60p series, '97.
- *Sandman* - Old Enough & Other Stories, Pont Young Adult Books, 1997, trans. to braille, National Library for the Blind, 1998.
- *Surfer & The Dreamcastle* - Sensational Cyber Stories, Doubleday, 1997.
- *The Chase* - The Young Oxford Book of Aliens, OUP, 1998.

Forthcoming Books

- *The Planet Machine* - SF adventure for 7+ year olds in A&C Black's new Comix series.
- *The Wintering - Ice/Storm/Thaw* - SF trilogy for 12+, Orion Books 2001-2002.
- *Storymaking Games* - games for developing literacy skills in the primary classroom, A&C Black, Spring 2001.

CONTENTS

She Bites

Her eyes said come and get me, her smile said don't you dare. And all of us in the school who were interested in such things vowed we would do anything for her. Eleanor Garou had moved to the area a couple of months ago and had been the centre of attention ever since, though nobody I ever talked to knew much about her. What I knew was what I could see, and I suppose that was enough...

She was tall - probably an inch over my five-feet-eight - and dark in a vivacious, secret kind of way; her hair, long and straight, shone with a deep blueblackness, yet seemed not to reflect any light; her eyebrows were sharp streaks, slanted a little to lend her a catlike look; her chin was pointed and not quite pert; her smile white and gleaming and always ambiguous. And her eyes...I always thought that she was looking out from somewhere way behind them, instead of through them, as though they hid big secrets; two-way mirrors on the world.

All of this had led me, and the rest of the football first eleven, to fall in love with her, brashly and competitively and definitely at first sight. It was not only the way she looked, but also that air of mystery she carried with her, and the fact that no-one had succeeded in taking her out all term, which allowed the rest of us to live in a hope that was not entirely vain.

She was clever too, never seeming to struggle for A-stars in termtime assignments, and she cruised through with top marks in all subjects when the exams arrived. Strange thing, none of the other girls grew jealous. Perhaps she flew the banner of the female cause too well for that, or maybe they knew that they'd just make fools of themselves if they tried to beat her.

In fact, the only kid in existence who must have disapproved of Eleanor Garou was a little squit in Year Eight called David Nimbley; class potato-head and also, alas, my cousin. I guess that was the sole reason I ever listened to him at the time, and possibly because he was also, in his own quirky way, as clever as Eleanor was. The difference between them was that Ellie had a wonderful textbook knowledge - often word-for-word perfect, whereas Dave knew all kinds of odd things; trivia, fragments, miscellanies of utterly useless facts that overlapped rarely on the real world of qualifications and a career in life. He understood about leylines and earth-magic, alchemy, Vlad the Impaler, quasars and pulsars and black holes: he could tell you how to survive in the Sahara using only what you carried in your pockets, or when eels migrate to the Sargasso Sea to mate: he knew how to blend the juices from garden plants to cure a headache or ease arthritis, or where King Arthur was truly buried, and he'd take you there too at a price...All pretty pointless of course, if you wanted to become an accountant or a computer programmer, as my parents insisted I did.

We were sort of friends and had been since early junior school days. I kept Dave from being bullied - lots of kids were tempted to push their fists into his pale bucktoothed face, just because of the shape of it - and he in turn told me how to protect myself against Wendigoes and divine for water if I was ever thirsty on a hillwalk. It was Dave who let me in on the fact that Eleanor was not quite what I imagined.

I'd stopped late one night for ski-training. The Human Potential Department arranged an annual trip to Austria in February, and I'd always had a hankering to go. I'd missed out so far (broken ankle in Year Seven, lack of money the year after that), and I was determined to make it before GCSEs got too much in the way of living. Exercise sessions began soon after the autumn term started, in early October, and became progressively more demanding until we were all so fit that skiing for six hours a day would, we were assured, be a pushover.

Anyway, I came away from school at six o'clock feeling pretty tired. All I wanted to do was get home, have some tea and then chill in front of the TV for the rest of the night. So when I saw Dave lingering around the main gate, I didn't know whether to run the other way, ignore him completely, or ask him what was wrong. Because something certainly was. I sighed and bit back my impatience.

"Hi Dave. What's up, man?"

He scurried across, sort of shrewlike, and put his arm through my arm as a young brother or a chaperone might do. His pale grey eyes were nervous and intense.

"Listen, Colin," he said, "you're in trouble. Big trouble, or could be if you don't listen. You understand?"

"If it's about the maths homework I copied off Specky Rowlands...Don't tell me the little squirt got every answer wrong!"

"Nothing like that." He glanced around himself; left, right, upwards. We scuttled across the road into the southern estate, making for home.

"It's about that girl, Eleanor Garou, in Miss Roberts's class."

"Now I'm listening."

"She's a vampire."

He said it in same tone he'd use to tell me that her star sign was Capricorn, or that she wore size seven trainers. I nodded, suppressing my smile.

"Right. I must stock up on garlic then and get hold of a stake. Actually, steak's lovely with garlic."

"I'm being serious, Col!"

"Yeah, and so am I. Now push off and go and turn lead into gold or something... Besides, how do you know?"

Dave stopped walking; stopped me walking and looked me straight in the eyes. Under the orange streetlight, his face was like a mask, one of those Greek Tragedy masks you sometimes see in drama books.

"Threads of evidence, woven together."

"Dave, I'm warnin' ya..."

"Her eyebrows meet in the middle. She never looks in the mirror, or goes near one. She stays indoors on sunny days."

"That's about *it* - "

"And I've seen her in St Mary's graveyard."

A light prickle of shock ran electrically along my neck.

"Give us a break... Short cut home," I snapped back defensively. Dave shook his head slowly, confidently, so that I felt like slapping him about a bit too.

"She has no home, Col. The address in the register says Plot Six, Lilith Way, on the new estate. Well there is no Lilith Way, not yet anyways. It's on the development plans in the town library, but at the moment it's just open waste ground next to the church. Plot Six abuts the cemetery as close as you can get without living in a long thin box. Oh, and the churchyard itself was closed in 1972. I checked."

"Is that it? Is that all you've got?" I asked, a little hollowly. Dave chuckled in triumph as much as with nerves.

"Well...I've watched her, followed her. She always uses the path across the graveyard. And - and she stares at the moon!"

"Good grief, I'm terrified... Wait a minute, so do you stare at the moon."

"I'm an astronomer and that's different," Dave replied, offended. "She just stares. And last time, two nights ago, she reached up for it and moaned. Honest, Col, I nearly wet myself."

Now my smile was wide and easy. He'd overdosed on daydreams again. It was getting late and Dave's face was sinking into the dusk, but I could see that he was still worried.

"She's got you really wound up tight, mate. Don't you realise that Eleanor must've guessed you were tailing her, and put that on just for show, simply to scare you?"

I flapped my hand at him and turned away. Turned back.

"Besides, why are you letting me in on this? I mean, I know I'm desperately in lust with - "

"I'll tell you why," he said with a quiet intensity. "Because she's after you, Colin." The words were short and stacatto, bitten off short with resentment and hurt. All the years of kids ribbing him had finally caught up, and the worm was turning.

"Rumours are already going round that she's a weirdo."

"Just jealousy, man. Plain and simple - "

"She's after you, understand?"

I grinned. "That's fine by by me. I might even let her catch me, after a little chasing around, you understand."

"Yeah, well." Dave shrugged. Under the orange streetlight his expression looked lost. "I've warned you and that's all I can do."

"Thanks Dave. I appreciate your concern. See you around."

"OK, maybe," he said with a wryness I didn't realise at the time. And then, out of the darkness as he walked away: "Just be careful, Colin. She bites."

*   *   *   *   *

"Hi I'm Colin Williams. Col to my friends."

I put my lunch plate down and sat opposite her, brash and big-grinned and tingling with anticipation; also nervous because of the way I'd dared myself to do this. People from other tables were glancing across. I saw Specky Rowlands nudge his mate's elbow and whisper something, born of jealousy no doubt, that would not be very flattering to me....

Eleanor looked up and smiled oddly: "So? Why should I call you Col?" She said it without speaking, and I felt instantly cold-shouldered. I started to tangle myself up in alternative plans.

"Um. Look, do you mind if I sit here? Um, please?"

"No, not at all." Her voice was velvety smooth and slow and husky. She brushed back her hair and returned to her meal.

"Hey, you like salad!" I nearly laughed with relief to watch her scooping coleslaw and lettuce on to her fork.

"Mmm. Keeps the hunger pangs away."

"Listen, em, Eleanor, isn't it? Ellie, I -"

I could hardly believe how I sounded: like a total amateur, a dork, bumbling my way clumsily through the approach while the surface of Eleanor's calm sophistication remained unrippled. And I nearly cried as my voice stumbled to a halt and hot embarrassment crept ruthlessly over my face.

"I know. You've seen me around, by myself, and you think I might be lonely. You'd like to think you could be my friend. Or maybe more. Fine. I'm free on Friday," she said quietly, with beautiful gentleness, and lifted her eyes to me. They were dark, glittering, gorgeous, impenetrable, reflecting all of my questions.

"Well, yes, actually, I was going to ask - "

"Let's call it a date, shall we - Col?"

I flushed again fiercely and glanced over at Rowlands. A victory glance.

"How about I meet you at seven? We could go to the cinema, or there's a play on at the theatre..."

"I'm not into amateur dramatics," Ellie said. "A walk maybe. We could get to know each other..."

"Yeah. Right. You live out on the west side of town don't you? I heard that..."

She nodded.

"I'll meet you by the church, then, at seven."

"Sharp," Eleanor said. Sunlight was coming in through the big panoramic windows along one side of the dining hall. And she didn't flinch once.

*   *   *   *   *

I found Lilith Way on the drawings in the library, and on Friday after school I checked it out 'in the field'. It was in the field too, very nearly - only a stretch of chewed-up ground that the diggers had been over in the summer, tufted with autumn-withered grass and littered with flints and broken half-bricks dredged up from long buried cottages. The ground had not been occupied for decades.

Just nearby was the graveyard, as Dave had said, and beyond that St Mary's church in its scrubby and abandoned grounds. Facing that way, north and east, the sky was gloomy; dark bulking shapes of yew trees rising against towering clouds that were another shade of deep grey. As grey as a gravestone. Westward the sun was low and near to setting, its last light all spilled out red and gold along the skyline.

I waited, and thought about things; this and that, in the lazy way thoughts come along in quiet moments. The lights of the town sparkled half a mile away, linking themselves to me by a single sparse row of lamps that defined the direction of the church road. It was empty of traffic. I began to feel distant and lonely.

What if Eleanor had been winding me up, as well? I wondered. Maybe she wanted to teach me a lesson - teach her other unwanted admirers a lesson too - get me shivering-scared out here so that I'd scuttle back to school and start adding fuel to the fire of Dave's stupid vampire theory. Perhaps that was her kind of humour, cold and cruel, preying on people's gullibility. Could be she was standing right close to me at this moment, watching me getting edgy, frightened, terrified.

I turned around, trying to be casual, as a breeze lifted the arms of the ancient yews and hissed in the laurel bushes that lined the gravel church paths.

Out of the shadows came a shadow.

"Ellie!"

"Sorry I'm late, Colin. I had to persuade my folks to let me out tonight. I was grounded..."

"No sweat."

To my huge pleasure and relief Eleanor whispered this close in my ear, and let her lips touch my cheek before she drew away. I heard her sniff at the cologne on my neck and shirt collar. Her hand traced a path down my arm and around my hand, and held it. My pride began to glow.

"I was getting worried."

"Sorry," she said again, facing me. She was night-dark, moon-cool and smelt of a strange perfume that slipped away out of my recognition the second I tried to identify it. From what I could see of her in the twilight, she wore a heavy pale jumper, bluejeans, dark shoes that might have been trainers; casual and practical, but they still flattered her.

"You'll get cold," I said. Eleanor gave a soft, deep laugh, brief as a sigh.

"I don't think so."

"Let's walk, then: keep the circulation going, eh?"

I was glad to leave Lilith Way behind. It was a name with no meaning behind it. Some developer's clever idea; probably named after his wife or his mistress.

"Where to?"

I was hoping for town, and began to steer her gently that way, but her hand answered by tugging back, away from the road to the church.

We passed beneath the lych gate and along the packed gravels of the path that made a rich crunching sound under our shoes. The sky was almost completely dark now, all piled up masses of black cloud with a few gaps between, through which the royal blue of the evening showed and a slash of blood-red sunlight: in one gap northwards glimmered a single fitful star.

Beside me Eleanor was silent. I could not even hear her breathing. We walked up to the looming hulk of the church and stepped under its porch. Then she spoke so suddenly that my brittle control shattered and my body tensed.

"See there!" She pointed to a triangular space between the lintel and the arch, a cut out shape of black. "It's a tympanum, put there to represent St Dunstan's fight with the Devil. There's a rhyme about it:

St Dunstan, as the story goes,
Caught Old Sathanus by the nose:
He tugged so hard and made him roar
That he was heard three miles and more."

She giggled lightly. "Can you imagine that sound!"

"No," I muttered, and wouldn't want to try.

"Come on." Ellie unlatched the heavy wooden door, pushed it aside and took me inside. The church was a place of emotionless cold. It smelt of old stones, stale candlewax and the faint fustiness of the damp carpets that lay along the aisles. The walls breathed out echoes.

"Spooky," I said, hushed, and the air sizzled with the sound.

"It shouldn't be. A church is a holy place, a safe place, eh Colin? This one is Norman. It's supposed to be built on the site of an older church, Anglo-Saxon, that was made of wood and thatch. Stave-kirks they were called: long decayed away..."

I was struck by a powerful sense of absurdity. Here I stood, alone with the girl I'd wanted to date all year, a hot-blooded male all ready to prove myself... And we were talking about early Christian antiquities. I laughed, disliked the boom of noise, and shut up.

"Why are we here, Eleanor?" I asked seriously. I had arrived because of a chance, a dare and a fantasy but now it was real and my body was cold and what Dave had said weighed heavily on my mind.

Ellie faced me and moved close. The perfume of her again. Her cool breath near my mouth. Her body against me.

"Because I know that you wanted proof from me."

"Proof?"

"That what your cousin said wasn't true. Proof that your narrow little universe is good and right and just as you expected it to be. Proof that I'm not vampire. How can I be, when I'm standing here under the eye of the cross, not in agony, not withering to dead leaves in front of you. Do you think I'm some kind of freak, Colin, like the others think?"

I felt ashamed and brushed aside my alarm that Eleanor knew of my conversation with Dave. I put my hand to her head and urged her closer. Her hair was made of shadows. I kissed her and it was sweet and normal and good. I could see her. I could see her now, because of the new light.

"The moon!" she said, and took my hand and walked with me along the nave towards the eastward facing window of stained glass. "It's so beautiful," she breathed in a rapture.

Suddenly I was still not sure. Would she melt into a thing of wings and fangs at my side, glare with red eyes and that demon's grin I'd seen on a hundred late-night movies?

No. She stayed the same, smiling as we both watched saints and angels glow like rainbows in the patterns of coloured glass.

"I'm sorry, Ellie," I began, "I really am sorry about this."

"Ah," she groaned, "the cleansing moon!"

I wasn't scared at all now. I just held still, as though it was all meant to happen like this, as I felt the hairs crawling out of the skin of her palm.

*   *   *   *   *

Gurney

I want to write this down now, just after it's happened, because in six months I don't think I'll believe it myself. No-one will believe it anyway.

When you start at a new school, there are ways of making the transition easy on yourself. I know this because when my family moved up to the Midlands and I joined Year Seven at Beckford Comp, I thought hard about the problem and decided that the best way to avoid trouble was to sort of slide invisibly into the new routines. Making waves, trying too hard to be accepted or popular, only brings you to the attention of teachers just itching to make you feel awkward and foolish (even so, I couldn't help being noticed by the Physics teacher, who always, loudly and sarcastically, called me 'sunshine'). And being high-profile also attracts the bullies, the kind who like to have a crack against any new kid, simply to prove that they're tougher and stronger and better than you are.

I survived, suffering only one minor encounter with such a kid - Len Donovan, Year Nine. He came up to me one day, pushed me over and put his foot down across my neck as I lay there.

"Feeling lucky today, wimp?" he asked, thinking he was being really cool and clever.

"Len Donovan?" I croaked. "Naa, not after what I've heard about you..."

His sneer of arrogance and aggression moderated towards puzzlement, and became a little lopsided.

"Listen, people tell me you're the king around here, and I can see why. You're tougher than I'll ever be. Come on, do you think I'm stupid or something? I've heard you're the big man at the school..."

Someone nearby laughed at all this rubbish. I turned fiercely.

"You're disagreeing that Donovan's the best?"

The grin on a little blond boy's face switched off.

I turned back to Donovan.

"Anyway, you could flatten me in ten seconds or less. I'm not even worth bothering with..."

I shrugged, and there rested my case. Donovan seemed to ponder this hard for a while, then stuck out his square lower jaw and jabbed a big finger in my direction.

"Yeah, well jus' don't get out of line, OK?"

"Yeah, you know me, right?"

He drifted away like a pike in a pondful of minnows, searching after other less puzzling prey. Happily the kids who'd been watching all this didn't voice their suspicions. Even more happily, the incident caught the attention of Kerry Lewis who appreciated the brilliance of my ploy and did not see it as a complete coward's way out of trouble. My first encounter with her is something I don't intend to talk about here.

Sheer bluff is one method of staying out of trouble. There are others. But when Scott Gurney appeared at the school after autumn half term, he went out of his way to get noticed.

First off, there was his name, not designed to camouflage one safely within a class of Davids, Andrews, Simons and Peters. Secondly there was the fact that 'gurning' means making a funny face, something usually done by toothless old men at village fetes, when they've had a few pints of stout at the local.

Maybe Scott knew this, or maybe not: however much of a coincidence it was, he actually made funny faces to attract attention!

And he was good at it. He was not the best looking kid in the world - not even quite normal-looking in fact. He had pale, straight hair, not so much fair as just colourless, washed-out blue eyes that stared like a fish (one of Donovan's minnows, I couldn't help thinking), a big bulbous nose, thickish red lips and a large mole on his right cheek. The effect was strange rather than ugly, and it made him look unintelligent, though in fact his voice was crisp and articulate. He had brains, just didn't seem to know how to use them.

I remember the first time I saw him gurning. It was at break on about the third day back after the half term holidays. Scott was standing in the sun, looking bewildered or dreamy, and a few kids from his form were passing by. One of them yelled, "Hey Gurney, give us a face!"

And of course he did, and a crowd gathered.

I gathered too, mainly because I'd heard rumours of this trick he had. I was curious, and I felt sorry for him though I didn't even know him. I just knew his type.

"What do you want?" Scott asked, a smart voice coming out of a dull mouth.

"Make us laugh. Give us a funny face."

"He's already got one!" somebody shouted. Everyone guffawed. More came to watch the circus.

And he began. First he did what most kids can do, the pig-monster face; thumb and third finger pulling on the skin below the eyes, index finger pushing up at the nose. Not much response to that one.

Then Scott attempted a traditional gurning face, turning his eyes inward so that only the whites were showing, sucking in his cheeks to make his mouth pucker like the blowhole of a balloon. How he did it with a mouthful of teeth I didn't know - not then at least.

A few kids were leaving the loose fringes of the crowd, but more were joining the fun. We all had the feeling I think that more, and the best, was yet to come.

"Try a dog," came another request.

"Lovely with chips!"

People cheered and laughed and Scott smiled stupidly.

He tried the dog and the crowd fell silent. We all saw him do it, but no-one was able to say how: and when he stood before us and howled, a couple of kids moaned and one ran away, I hoped to fetch a teacher...

First he stuck his head forward so that his lump of a nose jutted out, then he sort of rolled back his lips to show deep pink gums, opened his mouth wider so that white teeth glittered in the sun. His canines seemed long and prominent. He hunched his back, drew up his hands like paws. He grunted, gave a bark. His ears seemed to be pointed now, just like a dog's ears.

People started to mutter, impressed and a little unnerved. A group of girls giggled uneasily, sounding exactly like I felt. The noise began to swell and then someone clapped. Applause crackled through the crowd with the speed of a forest fire, kids cheered. One yelled, "Now do Mr Meres! Go on!"

Any new people at Beckford found out about Meres in the first few hours. He was the deputy head, a short hunchbacked man who must once have been in the army: whiplash voice, perpetual scowl, hard unforgiving eyes. He hated kids as much as we hated him. But we feared him even more.

Scott chuckled, appreciating the challenge. His dog's face melted and he flowed easily into a beautiful mime of Meres. His back seemed to bubble up under his blazer into the exact shape of Meres' hump: he stopped, made his eyes freeze over, did something with his eyebrows so that they looked longer and darker. Scott's mouth tightened in. He said, "Now you brats, you will line up outside my office - AT ONCE!"

That was too realistic to be comfortable. The voice snapped and echoed back off the school buildings - not Scott's voice, but the dreaded sound of Sergeant Major Meres in one of his Armageddon moods. It shut everybody up as effectively as if Meres himself had been standing there.

No applause came this time, only a slow realisation spreading ever faster that Meres was there, fetched out by the kid who'd run away for help.

A silence descended, one of those silences that seemed to be made of fine bone china. Nobody wanted to look at Meres for fear of catching his eye. A few furtive glances slid towards Scott, who slowly came back to himself, straightened up, his teacherish scowl dissolving. Clouds drifted over his face and he was Gurney once more, just an adolescent dumbo in a dream.

But Meres had seen, and must have guessed what laffs were being had at his expense - maliciously on everyone else's part, for other reasons as far as Scott was concerned.

"And what do you think you're doing?" Meres snapped, the words as sharp as pistol shots.

"Pardon?"

"Pardon SIR!"

"Pardon...sir."

Some kids were departing, doing their best to pretend that they had only been there by accident, and certainly had no intention of standing around to watch the rise being taken out of Mr Deputy Headmaster Meres Sir Your Highness. A hard core of the stupid and the curious remained, daring Meres' wrath upon themselves. I suppose I counted myself as a little of both, watching as Scott was verbally beaten up and dissected, then grabbed by the ear and hauled off to The Office wherein, it was rumoured - always in a funereal tone - hung the heads of Beckford pupils unwise enough to cross Mr Meres before his back was fully turned.

Maybe it was my imagination, but as Scott trotted beside Meres with his head cocked ridiculously to the side, the ear in the little man's fingers seemed to soften like warm plasticine: soft and stretch so that Scott, if he'd wanted to, could have pulled free any time he liked.

*   *   *   *   *

As it happened, I got to know him just as news of his escapade was spreading around the school. He was put next to me in French, at the desk by the window with our backs to the class. My reason for being there was that my command of French amounted to one or two swear words I'd learned from the locals on a day trip to Boulogne, and an oily ooo-la-la whenever Kerry Lewis passed by. She was in the same group, but at the top.

I think that Miss Bethnick put Scott with me not out of any compassionate motive, but because the boy scared her. She had probably heard about what went on in the playground, just like everyone else had, and it worried her. It was true, too, that Scott was pretty weird to look at. Which is why she chose not to look at him, telling him instead to 'get on quietly with something' until she had a chance to test his vocabulary.

So we found ourselves together through our old friend serendipity. I waited until Miss Bethnick had finished giving out her instructions, and the class was humming busily, supposedly practising verbs. Then I nudged Scott gently to get his attention and said out of the corner of my mouth:

"Hi. I'm Ben. Ben Leech."

"Scott Gurney."

"Yeah, I know. And keep your voice down. Do you want to land in trouble again?"

He chuckled at that, a low and somehow sinister sound that made me shiver, despite the fact that the double desk faced a radiator, and my feet were propped against hot pipes. I could suddenly see why he gave some teachers the creeps. Just something about him.

"What did Meres do to you?" I wondered a few minutes later. Miss Bethnick had done the rounds and prodded us both in the back for our chattering and empty workbooks.

"Ruler across the hand," came the reply. I was shocked.

"He can't do that! Not in this day and age."

"Well he did," Scott said. "But it don't hurt, not if you hold your hand slack, like this."

He showed me, making a shallow cup of his right hand so that the flesh was ruttled and cushioned, the heel of the thumb uppermost to take the flat edge of the ruler.

I nodded - stopped nodding - and began to see that something was not quite right with his skin. Like his hair, like his face, the skin of his hand was pale and almost see-through, and it wasn't red and inflamed as it should have been, either. But there was another thing, something elusive about it that I couldn't quite -

Then Scott pulled his hand back as Miss Bethnick descended on us again.

"Is this the thanks I get for allowing you two to sit next to each other, hm? Well, speak up!"

"Sorry, miss," I began weakly. "I was only trying to make him feel at home."

"And you, Scott?" Miss Bethnick demanded sternly, her voice heavy with suspicion and disbelief.

Scott stared at her and smiled.

"Sorry, miss, he was only trying to make me feel at home," he said in Mr Meres' voice, I nearly creased up.

*　　*　　*　　*　　*

I found myself hanging about with Scott after that without really intending to. It was the curiosity thing again. The crisp smoothness of his voice by itself told me that the kid wasn't stupid. It was like he was far ahead of us somehow, not needing the ordinary kind of education that Beckford could give him, but arriving here anyway for reasons of his own.

Besides, I wanted to see more of his gurning.

I asked him about it one day after school. We went to Bevin's on the corner for sweets, then wandered slowly up the long straight length of East Street towards the top estate where I lived.

"Where'd you learn to, um, you know - make faces, Scott?" I asked him, right out.

"Always been able to do it," he said, easily able to chew a mouthful of gum and speak perfectly clearly at the same time. "When I was a little boy my mum said I could be anything I wanted to be in this life. Yep, and she was right." His rubbery lips turned up. "It's the only reason people want to know me, actually."

I began to protest. "Oh, come on - "

"Except, I think, for you, Ben. You're the only one who calls me Scott, for a start. Everyone else calls me just Gurney, or worse."

"Well," I said, "it's tough enough having no friends at a new school. I hated the first few weeks here."

"Yeah, but now you're accepted, one of the crowd. People will never get used to me."

"You didn't exactly go to much trouble to blend in. And why'd you take the bait and mimic old Meres?"

Scott shrugged, a fluid rippling of his shoulders. "I like to be liked. Who doesn't? And it's what I'm good at."

"Fancy the stage, eh? Showbusiness - being a star?"

"A star?"

"Never mind. Anyway," I said to stop the conversation rolling downhill. "If you're so good, impress me with something. Go on - "

"What would you like?"

"Miss Bethnick," I replied at once, testing him right from the start because she was sort of bland, not easy to caricature like Meres, who might have stepped complete from a Dickens novel.

Scott smiled, lifted his eyebrows a little, pursed up his lips and wagged a finger under my nose.

"Is this the thanks I get for allowing you two to sit next to each other, hm? Well, speak up!"

It was perfect! Horribly perfect. I hooted with laughter and knew I'd never be able to look our French teacher in the face ever again.

"Blobber Jones now," I suggested: Scott's head seemed to grow until it was a red full moon split by Blobber's silly ever-innocent grin.

"Dork," I said next - the idiot of the class.

"Gis a sweet..." Dork's sandpapery voice came back at once.

"Me."

I was scared as soon as I'd said it, but all of Scott's impersonations had been effortless, and I considered myself a difficult subject to copy. What was the limit of his talent?

This time, he turned away, bending his head so that I could see nothing of him. The afternoon had been cloudy, building towards rain. Now in the gloom the first speckling drops tickled my face and the backs of my hands: Scott's body was a grey bulk a yard from me. I began to dread what he would show me, but I had to see it too. I had to know.

Then he straightened, turning back, smiling, my face on his shoulders.

"Where'd you, um, learn to make faces, Scott?" Scott said, my voice in his mouth.

Maybe in the sunlight I could have seen faults, seen how he'd done it. This was more than a lifting of the eyebrows and a hunching of the back, something I'd never come across before. It was - not - normal.

I think Scott expected praise, or pride from me maybe. I guess he wanted me to be impressed. And I was, so impressed that I was terrified.

I stood the look in my own eyes for no more than three seconds, then spun round and ran full belt back towards school. A car coming down East Street with its headlights already on blared its horn at me. I took no notice. I just ran.

Behind me, and over the swish of the car passing by, came Scott's plaintive voice.

"See you Ben. See you tomorrow..."

Words that belonged to nobody at all.

*   *   *   *   *

I did the stupid thing, of course, and followed him home next night. Still, I suppose I was only coming up to the expectations of most of the adults who knew me.

I explained to Scott in the morning, in a blustering evasive way, that in the dim light the night before I could have sworn I was staring into a mirror, and that it had scared me rigid.

"Try it now and I bet I pick you up on all the faults."

Scott didn't try it, nor did he attempt any more gurning or mimicking that day.

He told me he lived out of town towards Draybrooke. I checked in his form's register and found his address as Manor Farm, Draybrooke - a place that I knew had been empty and shut down for years.

I deliberately lost myself from him in the corridor crowds at the end of lessons, but kept him in sight and tailed him at a good distance, past the War Memorial and the golf course and out along the Draybrooke Road.

After a mile he turned off towards Manor Farm, but walked by the padlocked entrance gate and on to a lay-by. Parked there was a big touring caravan - one of those 'Fifties looking ones with plenty of chrome trim, like gypsy vans - and a big Ford truck.

Someone was standing in the open doorway of the caravan looking back the way we'd come. Scott hadn't spotted me, I was sure, and neither had the person in the 'van.

But I didn't want to risk being seen... Being chased by two like Scott... The thought of what would be at my heels!

I waited until Scott was level with the lay-by, then turned and hurried home, glad for once to be back in the crowded centre of town, where people staggered home under boxes of groceries, or got caught in the five o'clock rush. And other small and normal circumstances of human life.

Next day he came up to me, finding me without any difficulty in the doorway where I was huddled out of the blowy rain. It was early, and three bells hadn't yet rung - the signal for the duty teacher to let kids into the school.

"Hey," he began cheerfully, "want a sweet?"

Scott's hand came out of his pocket clutching a much delved-in bag of jelly babies. He took one himself, stretched the jelly head between his teeth until it parted from the body, then popped the whole thing into his mouth. He offered up the bag.

I ignored it.

"You don't really expect me to carry on as if it didn't happen, do you?"

"It?" Some of the cheerfulness ebbed away from Scott's expression, like rubber easing back towards its resting position.

"You know what I mean - Gurney."

His eyes drifted away, not quickly with disappointment or shame, but with a slow heaviness. Tired eyes. He nodded.

"I know. I tried not to let it happen, Ben, but it always does. I always go too far."

"Why?" I had to ask it, even though it felt like I was causing the first crack in a dam wall.

"Dunno. Suppose because I think it makes people like me. You know. Everybody loves a clown."

"You can always see through a clown's tricks," I told him. "They're obvious and clumsy, been done a thousand times. That's why people laugh. You're just too good at what you do."

It sounded all very philosophical, but I believed then I was right. And I still do.

"You all kept at me to do it - you as much as any of them."

I knew it, and dreaded to think what I might have asked him to become if I'd not thought to put the brakes on now, to put an end to it.

"My mum used to warn me about it, about giving too much of myself away," he went on in a quiet way that sounded strangely final. "Although she said that I could be anything I wanted to be, above all else I was myself. Trouble is, no-one likes me as myself."

His smile came from faraway, too deep and too much a mix of self-pity and loneliness and defeat for me to sympathise with him properly or even fully understand. I knew then that big gypsy caravan out Draybrooke way was his home, and that soon he'd be moving on.

"Ah," I said, not wanting him to vanish thinking the worst of me. "You're not such a bad old mate."

I put out my hand towards his shoulder - and had it knocked away by another hand that was big and square and bony.

Donovan stepped into view between us. He'd sneaked along the wall and, for all I knew, might have listened to everything we'd said, though how much of the truth he'd guessed was another matter. He smiled his shark's smile, the smile of the one who has weaker kids at his mercy, looking evilly from one of us to the other. Then he noticed the sweetbag that Scott was still holding, reached out and took it without resistance.

"What else you got?"

I began to relax away from the terrible thought that Donovan knew all about Scott and was ready to exploit the fact. Even if he'd heard everything, we hadn't given away the secret in so many words. The stupid prat was just after sweets and maybe some money and perhaps a little revenge.

I played it casually, took the fiver I kept for emergencies out of my inside pocket, and offered it up to him.

"You?" Donovan's eyes swung towards Scott, who shook his head sort of dumbly.

"He's new," I cut in. "He doesn't know what you're after."

"Money, cash, moolah." Donovan held up his fingers and rubbed them together. "Enough of it to save you from getting mashed, understand?"

It was quite likely that Scott didn't either, because nobody would've been daft enough to say no if they did.

"Come on, I ain't got all day!"

Donovan's short-fuse temper flared up. He grabbed Scott's jacket lapels in his big knobbly fists and swung him round against the wall. I began to rummage for more coins.

Then it happened, suddenly and frighteningly. Scott's face seemed to blur. I got the impression of skin growing over bones that dissolved and coagulated, changing and reforming like time-lapse pictures of clouds. A vicious smile swam to the surface of that sea of change.

"Come on, I ain't got all day!" Gurney said in Donovan's voice, although now he had Donovan's face too, right down to the scatter of blackheads across his nose, that still swirled even now into place like specks in stirred milk.

Donovan grunted in surprise, then let out a scream and tried to step away.

A hand rose up, Scott's hand. It was as big as a dinner plate, as big as a dustbin lid. It clamped octopus-like over Donovan's screaming face, cutting off the noise.

It made me sick, to see a hand that size holding the boy's head like I'd hold an egg. Don't squeeze, Gurney, I begged in my mind: please, don't squeeze him.

But Donovan had fainted. He sagged in Scott's massive grip and dropped. We'd won the battle if not the war.

But we hadn't got away clear and free. Other kids were about now, with just ten minutes to go to the bell. Some had stood watching, a couple of them fringe members of Donovan's gang.

One of them called, alerting others. They all came running.

"Inside!" I shouted at Scott, eager to get him away, though not so worried now about what the gang would, or could, do to him. At the same time I battled with the door onto the corridor - stuck firm, bolted shut.

"Out of the way," Scott said - thankfully Scott again except for that awful hand, which clenched like a club and smashed easily through the six-mill wired glass to reach the bolt at the top on the inside.

Scott yanked the door open and we dived through.

We ran, meeting no-one, although things were more serious now. Children were shouting and yelling outside. I heard the duty teacher blowing a whistle to shut them up. Soon he'd learn all about Ben Leech and his weird friend, his monstrous friend: then the whole school would be alerted, the police called...Scott wouldn't last the morning.

At the end of the long empty corridor we stopped. My heart was thumping and I heaved breath in great drags. The echoes of shouting banged about the walls behind us, catching us up.

"You've got to get out Scott. I mean, right away from the school."

"Don't worry about me," he said, very calmly, just as if this happened to him all the time. And it probably did.

"What'll you do?" I wondered. He was about to tell me, too, when the air crackled and a hunched shape appeared up at the French Block end.

"Gurney! Leech! Come here at once."

Meres was scuttling towards us, infuriated no doubt by the shattered doorglass and all the fuss we'd caused.

"Move it Scott." I pushed him on. Half way down the corridor the first bell went, shrilling over our heads. We were opposite the bio lab, another locked door, but kids were starting to appear at both ends of the corridor, with Meres' ghettoblaster voice herding them before him like sheep.

This time Scott didn't hammer through the window. His right hand moved towards the keyhole, fingers pointing, lengthening ever more delicately. Three fingers slid right in, twisted, and clicked the lock open. His mum was right - he could be anything he wanted.

He pushed the door and stepped into the lab. I made to follow, but he stopped me. "No point, Ben. You're in enough trouble already. Anyway, I'm leaving now. You won't see me again."

"Not see you?"

"Well, you won't recognise me, OK? Leave it at that."

I nodded stupidly, trying to catch my breath, say goodbye, explain how I felt, all at the same time and in the few seconds before Meres reached us. I didn't manage any of it.

Scott put out his hand and shook mine. It startled me to feel that hand - ordinary, warm, human.

He turned, looked quickly around, and began to change...

Two seconds later Meres caught me, nearly choking me as he grabbed my collar and dragged me back into the corridor.

He barged past me into the lab; into silence and stillness, with a hundred eyes watching him from preserving jars and the locust cabinet and the fishtank.

"And where is that friend of yours?" Meres growled, attempting to wither my soul.

I shrugged, all innocence, too dizzy with amazement to be scared of the man.

"I don't know sir," I said, with absolute truthfulness.

*   *   *   *   *

I ran all the way to the lay-by that night, and as I expected the caravan had gone. And I have never seen Scott since, though of course he said I wouldn't.

All the same, it's not easy to take the world for granted any more, and I look with new eyes at the stones and the trees, at the birds, at the endless sky...

*   *   *   *   *

Catch

Reg Button didn't care about anyone much. Which was why I loved him. He was old long before I was born, most of his life spent in a past that I had never seen and could hardly imagine. His wife had died fifteen years earlier, his children were grown up and moved away. He had a house and a pension, some money put by and a lot of empty time left to him to spend as he wished.

We became friends not because he saw himself mirrored youthfully in me, nor because either of us went out of his way to be sociable. It was simply that he liked solitude and so did I, and on a cold, late September day at Pitsford Water, neither of us expected to meet a soul. I'd come down to the reservoir to get away from people; a bossy sister, irritated snappy mother, a Saturday boss who expected you to do a paper round for peanuts and thank him for it. Besides, things hadn't gone too well that week at school. I'd fancied my chances with Anna, took a week to build up the guts to ask her out and then had been stared at as though I'd caught green measles. Great eh, especially when later in the day I'd seen her with Royston Simms - a kid with about as much personality as a warped plank.

I decided to walk the three miles out to Pitsford, following the old railway cutting most of the way, as far as the bridge (which is no longer there). And the tracks have gone, taken up for the metal: even the gravel's been scooped away for re-use. Not that I mind, because the land has been left to settle back into itself and become natural again.

After dawdling through the labyrinth of brambles, pausing every few yards to stuff a mouthful of fruit, I got a move on to arrive at the water before one o'clock. I'd come to catch fish - not 'to fish' - that was about as boring as I could imagine - but to pick up the few trout I wanted as quickly as possible and spend the rest of the afternoon thinking, dozing, watching the grey rippling flatness of the lake, like polished iron in a wind that had in these past few days begun to smell of autumn.

I reached the reservoir with time to spare, turning off the road into the lane that took me through the village (no post office, one pub and six houses) to the great open grass slope that swept down to the waterline.

I went straight to my favourite spot, a deep clear backwater pool half hidden by rocks. It was fed by a stream draining off the hill, the water tumbling whitely over pebbles. Trout liked to gather there, enjoying the fresh, aerated water with its boil of bubbles. Maybe the movement of it made them sluggish or dazed, because it was always easy to prod them with my bits of dowel that had onion netting stretched between. Drifting reluctantly a while, those fish seemed to guess they were being hunted, and turned to swim for it, straight into the mesh. Then I'd haul them out, bash their heads on the rocks to kill them quickly, cleanly. And that would be that.

'Course, it was not allowed even though I had a licence to fish the water, and no-one would ever call it sporting, old man. But I didn't do it for sport: I did it to eat trout.

The reservoir was slightly choppy that day, with a few boats out, distant like slivers of drifting white paper. I cast a glance to make sure nobody was nearby or watching, then I stooped to net my first fish...

It was easy. I caught a big two-pounder within minutes, hauled out a second slightly smaller one soon after and got busy stalking a third. That would be enough. No point taking more than I wanted.

I saw the shadow cast over the water and heard the voice at the same time, and nearly jumped in with the shock.

"That takes me back, though I used ash-sticks and not them fancy bits o' stuff you got."

I whipped round, both guilty and angry all at once.

The old man was standing on the high bank to my left, with the cloudy grey sky behind: I had to squint to look at him properly. He looked like a fisherman: great baggy corduroy trousers and canvas-lined wellies, a big green waterproof that crackled when he moved, tackle box slung round one shoulder and his rod, all packed up now, hanging by its strap from the other. Damn! Just my luck. Now he'd fetch the water bailiffs out and that would be the end of the game.

At least, that's what I expected. But he simply stood and watched and I thought to hell with him. I turned back round to fish for my third trout.

"You used to do this, then?"

"Oh yes, years ago. Matter of neccessity then. Not for you though, eh?"

"No."

"Do it for sport?"

"No, for the taste of trout."

He chuckled at that, a sound worn smooth in his old throat. "Best reason there is," he said and, "My name's Reg Button."

"Philip Stevens - Phil." I broddled about with my sticks in the water for a moment longer, but I was getting stiff. When the third fish turned its heavy body aside from the drifting net, lazily like a bar of hammered lead, I stood up with a grimace and shrugged. Reg Button was smirking, his face all lines and creases, and suddenly it occurred to me that he didn't really look like a fisherman after all, but like something else that I couldn't quite put my finger on.

"You like trout too, then?" He nodded and I picked up the bigger fish and told him to stick it away in his box pretty quick.

"Thank you son. Saves me the bother. You'll share a spot o' lunch wi' me for that?"

"OK," I said after a slight hesitation. "I've got nothing else to do, man."

We sat on the grass slope some way from the rock pool and Reg delved into his box for a bag of sandwiches. The food was wrapped, but I made a face when I saw the Tupperware container rustling with maggots that he kept right next to it.

"They for your afters?" I asked with a sickly grin.

"Lovely spread on toast," Reg answered with no trace of mischief in his eye: they were pale blue eyes like a long-ago sky, and the whites of them had gone a bit yellow and wet. He had a big bulbous nose with burst purple blood vessels at the sides. I made a bet with myself that he used a huge red spotted handkerchief to blow it with.

"Here." He handed me a wedge of sandwich, two thick roughcut slabs of brown bread stuffed with yellow cheese and succulent slices of tomato. It was a man's sandwich with nothing delicate about it.

"Come on, don't you cut the crusts off?" I asked him in mock surprise. He smiled and his eyes twinkled as if to say stop yapping, start eating.

We tucked in.

Afterwards Reg shared his two-pint flask of tea, the strong dark brown liquid making the roof of my mouth feel like the inside of a furred-up kettle. And we talked, endlessly, which was ridiculous, because an hour earlier we had been complete strangers. Now we swapped yarn like old friends. I moaned on about school - petty problems really - and grumbled about my parents. Reg listened without saying much, nodding occasionally in a way that did not imply either agreement or disagreement. Sometimes he spoke about his own childhood. It sounded sepia, faded now and distant. Reg's voice was thick with nostalgia, a keen longing for summer afternoons that would never come again.

"Well," I said, my voice lazy in the thin sunlight that had made the afternoon as warm as it was going to be. "I've never bothered much about the past. It's gone, man. What's done is done."

"But what's never done remains forever undone," Reg said. I made my mouth screw up.

"Come again?"

"The past is full of lost potential. Most people have wasted their lives. Perhaps I've wasted mine."

"I hope you're not saying I'm wasting mine!"

Reg said nothing. I looked round too late to see him nod or shake his head.

"So, not keen on fishing?" he went on after a silence.

"Not much, not really."

"I'll show you fishing, son." He stood with a grunt. I followed him, shivering a bit now because the sun was close to the trees and the wind off the water had turned colder.

I asked him, "You live close by?"

"In Pitsford. Why, you got to get back home, Phil?"

"Naa, I got all the time in the world, me."

Reg's house was maybe the biggest in the village, an old three-storey Victorian redbrick with brown and green rooftiles and light blue paintwork now peeling. A tatty yew hedge ran the length of the frontage and down the side. The place loomed. It was not as neat and trim as the other houses in the village, but it looked lived in and a bit scruffy round the edges, like Reg himself. Which is why I took to it straight away.

He made some sort of mumbled apology about the state of the garden: didn't look too bad to me with its lime trees still brightly in leaf, well-used plot for vegetables, and grass summer-long, September-golden: the sort of garden where little kids never run out of adventures to play.

We went inside to a hallway that smelt of sweet tobacco. And the same smoke seemed to have stained the place honey-coloured, almost the sepia of Reg's distant past. There was a tall coat-stand with a place for walking-sticks and umbrellas, a mirror, and a small round table. I stood and stared. On the table was a green bronze dragon, a foot long, wingless, lizard-backed, aggressively beautiful.

"Chinese, from the Chou Dynasty," Reg was telling me. "Nearly two thousand years old as far as I can judge."

"It's brilliant...Must be worth a fortune."

"Probably."

Probably! I nearly dropped where I stood. The old guy had to he cracked to leave something like that lying about unprotected on his hall table. Hadn't he got it valued? Insured?

But now he was hanging up his waterproof and beckoning me into the front room.

The place was a museum, cluttered with glass display cases, boxes piled high in the corners, all roughly labelled with faded embossed tape. The room was dark with heavy curtains pulled half across, but despite the gloom my eye caught the grey gleam of weaponry; swords and knives, the white shine of bones, paintings of past ages with their strange perspectives hung on the walls.

It might of course have been forged, all of it; or

reproduction stuff, but somehow I doubted it. I had begun to know him and that told me that this vast miscellany of objects was real. Real and true like the old man's heart.

"This is amazing, Reg," I said quietly. "I've never seen anything like it."

He hum-hummed a bit with pleasure and showed me one of the swords.

"No," he said as I started to admire it, "not a sword. It's a scramasax, single-edged longknife used by the Anglo-Saxons. This is one of the bigger sorts. You can get them as short as nine inches. Look at the handle here, gold inlay, gorgeous workmanship. One of my better catches."

That's when I began to feel cold prickles along my neck. I thought that Reg might have been eccentric up until now - the rich reclusive kind of eccentric you read about in magazines. But the way he was talking made him crazy - or else something was happening that I could hardly imagine.

Reg leaned the sword - the scramasax - against a drab 'Forties double wardrobe and picked up an oval lump of bone about twice the size of a hen's egg. It was a carving, crude but powerful, of a girl's head. The features were simple and smooth and innocent. Reg smiled distantly as he handled it, turning it over and over in his hands. The surface of his palms was as brown and as shiny as onionskin.

"It's a portrait, one of the earliest you'll ever find. Cro-Magnon sculpture was rare, and most of it was religious. This is probably a sister or a daughter."

"Where'd you buy it?" I asked, almost aggressively sceptical.

"Found it, son. A long cast, this was, and a difficult one."

"What the hell are you talking about? Where, Reg, where did you find it?"

"Let's go fishing," Reg said simply.

I followed him out of his room of treasures into the hallway again and up the stairs. The light was going now, just deep red puddles of it in corners and strips of it cast on the walls. The house seemed to be bigger, less friendly, and I felt we were walking deeper into strange and hostile territory.

A half open door at the end of the landing showed me Reg's bedroom (stuffed with more of his priceless junk), but we went the other way, to a room at the back of the house.

This place looked less well cared for: the landing carpet was threadbare, the floral wallpaper faded and dull. The air smelt, not musty, but not far off it, kind of old: an earthy smell. The smell of history.

And over and above it all I could hear the sound of the sea.

"What is that, Reg?" My voice came out just above a whisper. Reg answered me by pushing open the big pine door of the back room. Night had come, or maybe it had never left. The room was very dark, and chilled with air that moved steadily in a strong draught across our faces. Here the sound was much louder, a huge and distant crashing of wave over wave; of breakers over pebbles on an unseen shore.

"I'm scared Reg."

He put his hand on my shoulder, a heavy and solid and calming hand. When he spoke his voice had changed: now he was like a kid again about to open presents on a Christmas morning.

"Don't be. Just take some care Phil. Do as I say. Now, two steps forward - that's it. See what's there..."

I strained to see. The darkness was not quite complete, and looking back I noticed a pale fan of natural light sliding in under the door, now shut. But besides that some far away and faint illumination was in the air around me. And because of it I could pick out a clutter of objects scattered in a ragged line on the bare floorboards at my feet; some sticks and lumps of soil, bent scraps of metal, a Coke bottle, other stuff I couldn't identify. The floor faded beyond this into darkness.

Reg squatted down and picked among this flotsam like a beachcomber, muttering to himself in disappointment, disgust - then in some excitement.

"Here's something." He scraped away a thin crust of grey mud with his fingernail to reveal a small imperfect disc of dull yellow metal. He pressed it into my hand.

"Souvenir. Roman I think, by the ear of corn symbol. Anyway, keep it safe. It's yours."

"What's going on here?" It wasn't that I was scared any more, just curious now, and beginning to get caught in Reg's excitement. He chuckled.

"You've got imagination enough to guess. Sit there, cross-legged is best. Are you cold?"

"Not really."

He walked a few steps away and came back with an ordinary fishing rod and another tackle box, like the ones I had seen him with before, but not quite the same.

Reg sat beside me, checked for snags in the line, drew the rod back and cast out. The weight sailed into the night and the reel spun with a zing of uncoiling line. I heard no splash, but the line kept going, farther, farther into the depths.

"What," I asked him wryly, "do you use for bait?"

He smiled. "Curiosity, son. Works every time."

"You've fished for all those things downstairs?"

"Every one of them, but you can never tell what you'll haul out. For every bit o' stuff worth keeping, there's twenty things I throw back - "

"Back to where they came?"

"Probably not - "

"Coins in coal!"

"Wha's that?"

"I read about it," I said. "People have found coins in coal that was millions of years old, and in 1961 in California, miners found what they thought was a sparking plug in a lump of fossilized stone. A guy called Charles Fort wrote all about this stuff."

"Ha, well I hope you're not blaming me? I don't suppose I'm the only angler along these banks."

I thought then that maybe I'd offended Reg, because he said nothing more for nearly an hour. At one point he passed the rod to me and went away.

I sat in that nowhere-place, in the near dark, listening to the sea that was not a sea, wondering what strange ships sailed out there and if they ever visited still backwaters like Pitsford - until Reg came back with two big white mugs of steaming coffee. He was saying sorry, and I said it too by drinking every drop.

We caught nothing that night except a rather modern looking bottle of green glass. I wanted to hang on to it, but Reg hurled the thing away.

"Useless rubbish," he said grumpily.

We never heard the splash.

*   *   *   *   *

After that, I visited the old man a couple of times a week. He always showed me some more of his treasures and any new finds, and then we'd go to fish. The winter drew on and so I never saw the back room in the daytime, and I think I never wanted to. I dreamed it might still be as black as midnight.

One time I asked him, "Why'd you do this Reg? Not to get rich?"

We were both muffled up in duffel coats and gloves, scarves and woolly hats. The cold was cruel and our breath smoked in the air. The sound of the waves was fiercer tonight, wilder than ever.

Out there - wherever it was - it must have been wintertime too.

"Nothing to do with money. Why do fishermen sit their Sundays away in any case? They like to catch, but thinking about the catch is just as good. Besides, this is better. Because you never know what's going to come along."

Reg was right about that. One night after I'd made about the best and longest cast of my life - and I was getting pretty good at it with all the practice - I felt the line stretch tight and the rod start to judder in my hands.

I called to him, panicking. "Reg, help me, man!"

I could feel some heavy, powerful thing thrashing on the hook, its wild movements communicated up through the line and the rod, which was now arced over like a rainbow.

"Reg!"

I screamed it. The thing was pulling with a terrible force, and I took a step forward helplessly. I'd stood up when the line had first tightened, but now I wished I hadn't. My boots gritted on gravel, slid an inch on mud.

"Reg..."

He came clumping over and with a swing of his heavy arm he knocked the rod out of my hands. My grip had been frozen to it, clamped in a panic to the cork, and my mind had been frozen too, unable to give the order to let go.

"It was alive! Whatever it was...it was alive..."

"There be dragons, lad," said Reg, grinning wickedly. I forced myself not to let imagination run free, or I'd be sick with the shock.

I bought him a new rod and reel for Christmas with my paper-round money. I'd been saving for a radio controlled car, but that didn't matter. It wasn't the most expensive tackle around, or the best, but he opened the package with tears in his eyes and blew his nose into a huge red spotted handkerchief. I smiled to myself when I saw it.

"You're a good lad Phil. You know I could always have sold one of my treasures to buy the fanciest rod in the country."

But we knew, we both knew, that it would have been just another possession.

For a quirky thank you, Reg took our photo together. He set up the camera, adjusted the shutter delay and hurried round to stand beside me, arm on my shoulder like a proud granddad. He had two copies of the snapshot made, and gave me one just after New Year. I stared at it. No photograph had ever been like this one: not because this was different, but because now, to me, its moment had become as much a part of the past as the Pyramids or a fossil shell or the world's first sunrise. Now is what counts. And now. And now.

"Thanks Reg," I told him from my heart. "I'll keep it for ever."

That was the last time I ever saw Reg Button. I was kept busy with schoolwork for a week - teachers always launch into a new term with great enthusiasm - and I didn't get round to Pitsford until the following Sunday.

We'd had some thick gentle snowfall on Friday: Saturday had been fine, but Sunday saw a shift in the wind to the northeast so the day arrived in the middle of a blizzard that only let up well into the afternoon.

By five all the clouds had been swept away and the sky glittered with stars like cut glass glowing in the moonlight. There was a full moon. Reg had said something about it affecting more than just the terrestrial tides, and so I was vaguely worried as I trudged the last mile into the village.

The worry sharpened when I reached the front gate. Something was wrong. The house, normally bleak, looked even more abandoned and empty.

I trudged through the snow piles and went into the house using the key that Reg had given me. When I shouted his name the house echoed with it emptily, but no answer came back.

I banged up the stairs and ran along the landing.

It looked as if a storm had hit. Fragments of soil, tufts of grass, leaves and twigs lay strewn all down the passageway.

The old-fashioned bowl of a lampshade above the stairwell had smashed, its glass lying like curves of pale eggshell on the threadbare carpet.

I walked into the back room and a blustery east-coast wind swept sand grains up into my eyes.

The room was a shambles. Large chunks of wood and fist-sized stones were scattered all about. One thick stump of a log looked as though it had been hurled into the wall by the doorway, dislodging wedges of plaster. The sea roared. And at our fishing place Reg's tackle box lay overturned, and the handle and a two-foot length of his rod, snapped off sharply; the top section, weights and line were missing.

I will never know exactly what happened. Perhaps the storm was too much and swept him out, or maybe the dragons from the bottom of the ocean came rising through the depths as Reg sat and dozed away his hours on the lonely shores of eternity. He was a solitary fisherman. No-one else was there to help him that night.

I carry on, visiting two or three times weekly, letting myself in with the key Reg gave me. No-one notices, there are no suspicious looks or questions asked.

And there is always the chance that I'll find him again, washed up somewhere, or floundering in a limbo of nothingness. I'll keep on until people discover that Reg is gone, and his house is sold and its treasures are scattered. And what a stir that will make in the papers!

I'll keep at it, though I've cast far and wide and deep. Sometimes I wonder if you can swim in this sea, or sail in it to summer afternoons I thought might never come again. But I haven't tried that yet, I haven't dared. For deep down I know that the waters are dark and the tides are uncertain.

*　　*　　*　　*　　*

Dragon's Egg

Looking back, I don't know which bit was stupider: falling in love with Hayley Masters, or ignoring Austin and his dragon's egg. I suppose I didn't believe in either quite enough.

It had been a warm early September after a grey washout of a summer: lots of county cricket rained off, a barren wasteland on the telly, and farmers complaining that their harvests would be down on previous years. Nothing memorable stood out from the great stretch of the holidays, and it was only on going back to school and into Year Nine that things started to happen.

One: I was picked for the soccer first team, Belter the games master deciding that I'd played well enough in house matches last season to qualify for 'a coveted position' on the left wing. He made it sound like I'd just joined the England squad, but I let him pour on the praise as well, even though we both knew my talent was mainly aggressiveness and turning up reliably for training sessions. Still, it was better than a kick in the teeth, as my dad was so fond of saying.

Two: I befriended this kid called Austin Williams. Don't ask me why, because even now I couldn't tell you. He had a maniac little brother whose name was Manfred, and they lived together with their mother who was about thirty-six, but who looked fifty, Father having packed off several years earlier when life, I suppose, crossed some sort of threshold for him into nightmare.

To be fair, Austin has always been a good mate since we first sat together in our new maths group (set four), but his loyalty was sometimes irritating and his dreams so vividly imagined - and explained to me in such detail - as to be frightening.

Fact was, he lived in another world in his head. Many teachers told him that, often crossly, right from the start. 'Daydreaming doesn't get you through exams!' I thought it was just one of those expressions, part of a kind of ongoing reprimand for scrappily finished work. But of course, Austin didn't care. I mean, if you exist in another dimension teachers must seem as ephemeral as shadows cast by sunlight on a cave wall.

Three: I met Hayley Masters, and from then on thoughts gathered naturally around the image of her face.

She was tall and mature for her age: intelligent and very pretty, despite the wire brace on her teeth, which would come off in a year or so anyway. And her hair was black, and it came down to her waist: didn't just hang there, it swirled. It was alive.

I knew she'd noticed me during, I think, the second English lesson of the term. We were reading some book, and the phrase came up: 'She gave one of those taunting smiles that made him go weak at the knees.' Pretty corny stuff, but my eyes lifted from the book and I found Hayley looking right at me across the width of two tables. Her smile was not taunting, in fact it was barely there at all: but her gaze was dark and clear and I realised that sayings are often cliché because they're true. I stared her out with great seriousness, until she coloured and looked away. But contact had been made: she was inside my head and it was, as they say, lurve at first sight.

I thought I could do nothing better than hang around at the school gates after last lesson and maybe catch her as she went home. A mate of mine said she was new in the town, having moved up from Kenniston during the summer.

"Get in quick, Kev. Half the male population of the school's out for the kill."

I believed it too, and although I'd never gone in for

chasing girls, the thought of my arm around Hayley's shoulder on the way to some disco, or walking in the park, made my heart pound harder than if I'd run a pitch-length and back.

So I leaned against the white gatepost in the forecourt and tried to look casual while crowds of neatly-uniformed sparkly-eyed little Year Sevens milled all around me.

Just my luck that Austin found me before Hayley appeared. There he was, standing right in front of me, face upturned and a big gap-toothed grin stretched across it. He looked like something put out for the bin-men: scraggy shirt all frayed at the sleeves and grubby around the collar, grey school trousers sewn with blue thread at the knees, and at half-mast showing green luminous socks underneath.

"Hi Kev, howya doin'?"

"Go and play with the traffic, Austin," I said without looking at him. Hayley had come out of the Art Block and was crossing the central playground in my direction.

Austin tugged at my arm. "Hey Kev, I want to show you a place"

"Will you clear off!"

"But I've found a dragon's egg."

"Yeah, later, later."

I saw Hayley half turn as though someone had shouted at her. She paused, and Steve Connell strode up all macho swaggering and - do you believe this - carried her books for her! It made me want to vom.

"Damn," I said, outwardly cool above a rising fury. "Damn and – what did you say?"

Austin was staring vaguely in Hayley's direction, wondering what the fuss was about. "Dragon's egg," he repeated casually, and with an undertone of hurt pride. He held a fragment of something for me to look at.

I took it from him; a scrap of what seemed to be smoothly milled aluminium about the size of a playing card, but roughly triangular, curved and with snapped, ragged edges. It was light too, and thin, but so strong that I was unable to bend or break it. Spots of dull yellow speckled its outer, convex surface.

"If you hold it into the light – " Austin started to explain, then moved it himself, tilting the piece of stuff until the greyish colour shone matt-metallically and the gold speckles gleamed.

I was fascinated, more by the mystery of what the thing could be, rather than because I believed it was what Austin said it was. Maybe it was from some machine or other, but at the same time it was oddly natural: a strange cross between something manufactured and grown.

"That's only a bit of shell, of course." Austin was superior now, almost snooty. "I can get lots of those. What's really good is the whole egg I found with them. Whole and unbroken."

"Where?"

Hayley and Connell walked off together down the road. Faintly, just before they turned the corner, her laughter filtered back on the warm afternoon air.

"I'll show you," Austin told me, giving nothing away. "After tea."

❉   ❉   ❉   ❉   ❉

It turned out to be Rowland's Wood, a straggle of oaks on a hillside about five miles out of Rossborough on the Lenton road. Although the day had been fine and sunny, hazy cloud had thickened steadily so that by six o'clock the sky was heavy and yellow with bluish thunderheads swelling in the south.

We made fair time - even with Austin's skinny legs and pedalling on his sister's bike which was about two sizes too small for him. He kept up bravely, but we were both sweating at journey's end, an itchy, uncomfortable sweat in the dry pre-storm heat.

"It's private land," I pointed out. We propped the bikes against the hedge: not many cars came this way. "What were you doing here?"

"Often come here. At Midsummer and Hallowe'en, or whenever I can really. I like it: it's quiet and nobody ever walks through the wood, no farmers or hikers or, you know, couples... It's like part of the Old World: nothing to do with cars and science, or TV or towns."

"'Old World'?"

"The world of enchantment and magic," he said in all innocence and with absolute sincerity. "Where beliefs can really cause things to happen."

"Austin, my son, you are weird!"

"Yeah, right. In a past life maybe I was an alchemist or a wizard or something."

Or village idiot. I thought it, didn't say it.

We followed a dried out twist of pathway about a hundred yards into the wood before Austin indicated we should strike off at an angle.

He broke through a screen of bushes and the light faded at once as the leaf canopy thickened over our heads. Our shoes crunched on fallen acorns. A whippet of branch swished back across my face with a stinging smack, and in the distance the first thunder grumbled like some huge animal just waking up.

"This is stupid, Austin. We're going to get caught in the storm and drenched. Or struck by lightning, knowing my luck!"

"We're nearly there, at the middle. You don't expect dragons to make nests out in the open, do you?"

"Well no – But I mean, the whole thing's stupid. Dragons don't exist, man. It's make-believe, Austin, get me?"

"Make-believe. Making beliefs. Dragons are grey," he said softly. "At least, they are in Europe. Chinese dragons can be green or red: in Scandinavia they have a blue colour, like heated metal. They can eat fruits or wood like many other animals, but they like to crunch stones, especially if they have iron in them."

He smiled. And that's what frightened me. At least, that's what I thought it was, until Austin suddenly stopped.

"The centre of the wood," he said, cocking his head as though to listen. "Six ley lines cross here. It's a powerful node. Can you feel it?"

I could feel something: the faint ozone-prickle of the air perhaps, or just the sheer stillness of the place. But he was right. Something. Something.

Just then the world blinked, a pinkish flash that washed out all detail and colour; lightning split the second.

During the interval between brilliance and sound, Austin moved quickly to a big old tree in front of us: its heart was rotten, the trunk split and covered with orange flanges of fungus. Erosion, or something, had exposed its roots like a handful of clutching fingers. Austin scrabbled between them, flinging more scraps of 'shell' about in a panic, until his body relaxed and gently, oh very gently, he lifted out his dragon's egg and held it up like a trophy.

I thought this was either the best practical joke in the world, or he'd found some strange species of fruit, or a gall or whatever… Or he'd discovered the first ever dragon's nest. Miss Whiteside our biology mistress was going to be pretty amazed at this, one way or another.

Austin grinned briefly, triumphantly, but as the wind rose to thrash through the topmost branches his face changed, turning serious.

"Dangerous now," he said in a breathy whisper. "Let's go back."

We ran, hurrying like a couple of thieves the way we'd come, taking advantage of gaps in the undergrowth and then the track leading back to the road. Coming out of the wood was like stepping into a warm, dark room: a sky shadow-black and bulging with evil clouds, the wind dragging willow-herb heads into drifts of fluff and sweeping flurries of leaves towards town.

I knew something was going to happen. I guess in the same way that Austin could feel the nodal point of the wood. My first premonition.

Our bikes were where we'd left them, casually leaning and untouched. I noticed that Austin's had a wire basket at the front, lined with screwed-up newspaper, as though he'd planned to bring back this treasure all along.

A fresh gust brought a warm splatter of rain, high-summer rain languid and fat. More lightning was building behind the sky: I flinched a moment before I needed to – flash-flash - forks of light that looked like the oak roots where the dragon eggs had been. Or whatever they really were.

Austin's thin shape seemed etched on the picture of the land. Then he staggered, nearly dropping his prize. It was round, like a turtle's egg, beautifully formed and smooth. I was suddenly afraid he would drop it: afraid of what might come out.

I jumped forward, one hand steadying his arm, the other cupping the metallic sphere.

It was humming, ever so faintly, like a very efficient motor.

"God Almighty." The thing was alive.

*   *   *   *   *

We got drenched, as I'd anticipated. We freewheeled into town through a sizzle of roadwater, went straight to my house and hid the egg under a pile of magazines in my den at the bottom of the garden. Actually it was a shed that none of the family had bothered using since we'd moved to the house three years before. I'd offered to clean it out and creosote it, and then maintain it if it could be my den. Neither Mum, Dad nor Sue argued. I even had a padlock on it now.

"It'll be safe here," I told him. "I've got the only key." Austin nodded, but vaguely, like his thoughts were far away, seeing things that normal people did not think about seeing. There was one kid in Year Eight who was a real UFO freak: kid called Jeff Collis. He kept spotting lights and 'saucers' in the sky, and then went round telling his (pitifully few) mates that an invasion was imminent. He had even hinted that he was a Martian himself, but this was a dark secret never to be made truly public. The fact that the whole school knew and strenuously avoided the boy hardly mattered.

But Austin was different. Despite all the names I called him he was not mad, nor the sort who'd do or say anything for attention, even if it took the form of derision. To tell the truth he was pretty ordinary really; average, but when he daydreamed, you wondered how real those dreams might be to him.

"I shall want to visit it," he said, gently demanding: "Every day."

"OK, sure. No problem." I even considered giving him the key, not wanting to be involved in whether the whole thing was true or not.

"Every day…"

"Yes!" I saw Mum watching from the kitchen window and wiped the expression of irritation off my face. "Fine. Every day. Spot on."

"Because," Austin continued, "I'll need to prepare. For the hatching."

*   *   *   *   *

Over the next couple of weeks I even managed to forget all about the affair on one or two occasions, usually those times when I was actively on my mission to date Hayley Masters. The presence of Steve Connell was annoying: well, actually it drove me up the wall and round the bend, but the kid was too much of a creep to be a serious rival. Hayley, very coyly but with great expertise, played us off one against the other; never telling him outright to clear off, always cleverly avoiding my efforts to pin her down to a date.

I soon realised that she was waiting for the next big occasion on the school calendar, the mid-term disco. Since I'd been at Rossborough the dance had served as a late settling-in social and an early celebration of Hallowe'en; meaning that the Head of Year and staff only had one lot of organising to do. But they normally made a good job of it and the disco was always a huge success.

It was also something of a showcase. People who went and were noticed were talked about, sometimes enviously, sometimes bitterly, sometimes fondly. The dance formed the big gossip-generator of the year. And relationships that survived for a week afterwards tended to last. Don't ask me why, but it's true.

I thought hard about how I'd fit with Hayley, and she with me, and I reckoned we were a good match. I'd had enough of one-week, two-week relationships. Hayley was interesting, deep and still. I'd enjoy getting to know her.

Meanwhile Austin had been as good as his word, coming round daily to tend to his egg. At first I'd go down the shed with him and watch him lift the thing reverently, almost soothe it with his hands, and put it carefully to its ear as though listening for its wisdoms.

I'd tease him, of course, I think through a mild embarrassment that anybody could be so intense about something that was supposedly legend and myth. One time I nudged his elbow and chuckled at his panic as the sphere wobbled in his hands.

"Steady Austin, might be an unexploded bomb."

There was no temper in him, no smart comeback. He simply looked at me and smiled, such a knowing yet veiled smile that it frightened me. I tossed the key to him, acting as casually as I could, and didn't go near the shed again.

September went out warm and windy, but the first week of October was cold, with plenty of rain. The term had settled, I dealt with schoolwork steadily, as it came, under no pressure.

It seemed no time at all before the air began to dance with talk about the disco, and rumours took root and grew – often alarmingly and sometimes disastrously. Connell began to hang around Hayley more frequently and more intrusively. I let him make an idiot of himself with his fawning, and held back, judging my time almost to the hour.

With four days to go, I caught Hayley at the end of school and pitched the invite. She knew as well as I did that my intention had always been to ask her, and I guess we both knew what the reply would be. But she hesitated, staring shyly at the ground: all part of the ritual.

"You know that Steve has already asked me…"

"Oh yeah?"

"Four times." The hint of a smile.

"I'm only asking once," I said. Big talk, but my heart was racing.

"He said he'd come anyway, whether I go with you or not."

"And are you going to?"

"You know how I feel... I'll see you at the dance."

The time came round in a flash. I saved up from my Saturday job and bought a new pair of chinos which went great with my blue JA modal shirt. I felt good all that week, glowing with pride, but not sure if it was a grown-up feeling or one that was deepdown childish and mean. I ambled through my work and didn't care for once when it came back C-graded or worse.

And the future felt stable and sure; the thought of dancing with Hayley like a solid base on which my happiness rested. Beyond that? Well, you never knew. But I had my hopes and my dreams

Friday sailed by, the school day seeming like a brief diversion between the excitement of getting up and the deeper anticipation of the dance.

I didn't bother to check things with Hayley. She'd given her word and she knew I'd turn up. We had an understanding, a good first step. And neither did I trouble to visit the school hall at the end of the day to look at the decor, which I had done in years past: I wanted it all to be fresh that night, gleaming and colourful and fresh. I wanted the whole impact to come at once.

By six o'clock I was ready, although no-one even turned up until seven at the earliest. Mum knew better than to fuss me after tea, and Sue knew better than to tease. She'd had important days like this herself, private days ultimately, because so much of your soul was showing in public.

So I just sat in my room gazing out over the back garden,

and the gardens beyond, and the sky which was a moving grey-black mass of clouds dragging its sheets of blustery rain.

I stayed for nearly an hour, watching, thinking.

Close on seven Austin turned up, a gawky little figure in a green duffel-coat ludicrously too small for him. He unlocked the shed and went in. The door slammed back in the wind.

It was almost impossible to stir myself at last now that the moment was here; go downstairs for my jacket and step out through the front door into the street. I had gone over the possibilities in my mind time and time again, planning aftermaths, so that actually setting out to achieve them now seemed troublesome.

The wind swept up the house-side spitting rain in my face. The sky was already dark and streetlights were coming on. I called a vague cheerio to the family in general, pulled the back door shut - and saw Austin frantically waving at me from the garden. I made exaggerated mimes of pointing at my watch, shook my head and set off. His voice followed me, a distant wailing plaintive and small. Why the hell now!

I paused at the gate, struggling with the dilemma of what I should do, long enough for him to come running up. He almost fell against me, panting, gulping air so that for a moment he couldn't bring himself to speak.

"Trouble!" he said at last. "It's hatching, Kev. Now. But..."

His eyes were like sparks, with the skin had stretched taut and white around them.

"But what?" Anger and apprehension mixed up together. I wanted to push him away.

"It can't manage by itself. We need help, Kev..."

"I've got to go. I can't let Hayley down, man –"

"Please!"

And he began to cry, a totally hopeless sound, stupid little sobs and sniffles. He just stood there. And his nose started to run.

I ran back, swearing all the way, not caring if Austin was behind me or not: past the lawn that was now leaf-littered and scrappy, down the side of dad's veg patch and into the shed.

It was hot in there, hot like a blacksmith's shop, and it stank like one, of cinders and scalded iron. The egg rested on a bed of gently glowing sparks. Austin came in behind me.

"It's trying to get out, Kev, but can't. It's not strong enough. Listen."

Imagine a nail drawn down glass, a scrabbling of many such nails. That was the sound, but somehow softer and quite weak. And under that noise, a small pig-like grunting mixed with a mournful keening very high up the octaves; painfully high.

The dragon was inside, ready to be born, but not able to free itself. It was going to die in there, before it had its one chance of life.

I rooted about on a shelf and found the penknife I had once used for whittling – a past hobby. It was one of those expensive Swedish Army knives with lots of blades. I crooked open the stoutest blade, bent over the egg (it was like leaning your face above an electric fire) and tried to make a cut. The shell was harder than steel.

I tried again, this time looking for a fracture or some blemish in the sphere. Sweat began prickling on my skin. A drop of it hit the shell and faded.

I found the crack I wanted, used a newspaper to protect my left hand as I held the egg steady, and levered with the knife in my right. I had to use all of my strength even to drive the blade further. And then suddenly it snapped with a loud ping and shot off into a corner. But a fragment of shell had also come away, leaving a half-inch hole. Steam or vapour lifted from inside, and in the darkness of the egg I saw something glowing. It was curved, textured like golden satin, a beautiful swirl of shades like the surface of a soap bubble. It was the baby dragon's eye.

That stopped me dead. It was nothing like looking at a human's eyes, or an animal's. It was neither. No, it was both.

I stepped away. The eye vanished and a tiny black claw probed through the hole and picked futilely at the edges.

"It's no good, Austin. The thing's had it. It just can't break that shell, neither can you. Neither can..."

"It's a dragon, Kev. What did I always say? It's a dragon... He whispered this without any trace of gloating, sensitive to the shock of my acceptance.

"It's just no use. It's just going to die." I shrugged and handed him the knife.

I went outside and let the wind bring me back, as though I had stepped into a pool of icy cold water.

     ✳   ✳   ✳   ✳   ✳

I was late to the dance, over an hour late because I had not gone straight there. Instead, I'd wandered around the long way, through estates and the town centre rather than cutting across the Rec. Everybody had turned up of course, and chart music bumped and clattered above the sound of laughing, chattering groups. Hayley was there. Her eyes were searching, though when I walked in she turned straight to Steve, giggled overloudly at some no doubt stupid comment he was making, and proceeded to ignore me completely. Steve took advantage of her mood to drape his arm over her shoulder and nuzzle into her neck.

And she has ignored me ever since. I hung around for ten minutes, magnetically caught between pleading with her and taking Steve outside to slap that inane smile off his face. I did neither. I hurried home and went straight down to the shed.

Austin had left. The place stank like an old bonfire, though there was little trace of damage. The air was thick with stale smoke and a mildly sulphurous tang that I both tasted and smelt, a little of each.

Dragon shell lay scattered on the floor, together with droplets of liquid that looked heavy and scarlet, metallic like mercury. I thought about cycling out to Rowland's Wood, where maybe Austin had gone to bury the stillborn thing, or perhaps to release it if it had lived.

He never told me, one way or the other, nor even speaks much when I'm around any more. He still looks distant and vague, seeing what is not in front of other people's eyes. Hayley and Steve are into the third month of a deep and lasting relationship, all neatly sewn up and complacently secure.

And me? What was plain and simple, clear and easy to understand, is not so now. I deal with schoolwork steadily, as it comes, under no pressure. Days go by, as they used to do. But the difference is that I don't know what to look for any more – what might be true and what make-believe; a tilt of black hair in the crowd at the school gates, or the gleam of a metal-grey wing in the moonlight.

*　　*　　*　　*　　*

Brag

At first, Ben Peterson was one of those kids I just didn't like. We hang around at the same youth club - the Gemini Centre in town. That's where I met him. Plenty of kids like me started going to the centre to keep out of trouble...Never mind what sort of trouble; but if I'd carried on the way I was going, I reckon I would have been slammed up and off the streets by now, and that's a fact.

Anyway, all that's important to know is that Mr Sellers talked me into dropping by one time, and things got better from there. Sellers was my games master when I was at High School, and the only teacher who never took any backtalk off me. In fact, in Sellers' lessons I was a good little boy; good as gold. I didn't resent that or anything, because although Sellers was tough and had a voice like a cannon going off, he was also fair. With him, you knew where the lines were drawn. That's why he came down hard if ever you stepped over them.

Mr Sellers made me welcome at the Gemini Centre. He was there most nights, joining in and organising stuff for the kids who came round - and not just talks about staying off booze and drugs: there were all kinds of other things going on too, like entertainment. Sellers seemed tireless in his wish to help out, to genuinely try to show us that we could make decent lives for ourselves. I asked him about that once, and he took me aside to a quiet corner and laid it out plain and simple.

"Steve, I've met plenty like you - young men and women full of anger and frustration. I guess what's happened in your lives has made you what you are; broken homes, pretty awful time at school. Maybe you feel the system has let you down - am I right?"

I shrugged casually, which meant of course that Sellers was dead right, and knew that we both knew it!

"Fact is," he went on, "you've survived. You're here tonight listening to some old fool lecturing you about the right way to live. But don't worry, I'll clear off in a minute or two... All I want to say is that you're old enough to take responsibility, Steve. And by taking responsibility, you'll soon be able to take control in your life. Make some decisions, do something to help yourself - "

"Like what?" I asked him, sort of sneering. And then Sellers told me the real purpose behind the Gemini Club...

"It's a kind of a buddy system. I match you up with another kid of about your age, someone who's maybe turned up here once or twice but looks as though he'll drift away again and not bother. I'd ask you to take responsibility for this person when you're here. Be welcoming, show him around, involve him a little. We got plenty to do here - what do you like doing here, Steve?"

"Well..." I grinned sort of sheepishly, having to admit it. "I spend most of my time on the videogames machines. I think, um, it's really the only thing I'm good at."

"OK, show your buddy how to play. Teach him to be as good as you are. And don't put yourself down about it. Who knows where an interest in videogames might take you? You just never know, right?"

I shrugged again, then said, "You keep saying 'him'. Any chance that my buddy could be sixteen, female, blonde and built like - "

"You make your own dates," Sellers grinned, wagging a finger at me. "But come along on Friday and I'll have arranged something that might be an incentive to you..."

The 'incentive' was a pair of new games machines, state of the art. I heard later that Sellers had talked some local businessman into sponsoring the hire of them for a year. Furthermore, all the money that we put into them, once the rental was paid, got ploughed back into the Gemini Centre for further amenities. I didn't think that would work, until both machines jammed up after the first week, and it was found that their coin boxes were crammed with money. And thus, Sellers went up another notch in my estimation...

On the downside was that my buddy turned out to be Ben Peterson. He looked like a real wimp; tall and stringy with curly fair hair and a whipped dog expression he wore most of the time. I'd seen him at school, once picking up some hassle in the playground - because losers like him just seem to attract trouble, you know: the harder they run from it, the harder it pursues them. Well, it wasn't my problem then, so I don't feel guilty about it.

Sellers introduced me to Peterson and the games machines at the same time, suggesting that spending half an hour or so on them might be a good way for us to get to know one another. Sellers dug in his pocket and dropped five pound coins into my hand, then left us to it. Sheer blackmail of course, but very effective.

"You ever play on these things before?" I asked Peterson. He looked at me, then at the machine, then at me again, and gave me a slug-eating grin.

"Naaa. It's kids' stuff, innit?"

I could have fat-lipped him there and then. But remembering Mr Sellers' mission, and the kindness he'd shown me, I just tutted, slid a quid in the slot, and chose my scenario...

It was Alien Berserker, a favourite. Created by the U.S. games company KillWare, Alien Berserker was the best you could get in simulated shoot-em-ups. You could learn to play from scratch, or pick up advanced new skills, by reading a scroll-down screen that gave a concise overview and/or which took you through demos of the controls and sample missions.

Basically, having chosen your spacecraft and weaponry, you launched into deepspace from Earth Conclave and sought out the invading alien hordes that made the universe such a naff place to live in. Once you found alien clustercraft, or a swarm of the creatures on some inhospitable rock outpost, you blasted them to dust.

Sounds gratuitous, but the game incorporates training sessions, and up to thirty missions grouped into six separate campaigns; each campaign featuring a different alien species - but all of them intent on dicing-and-slicing the human race.

I showed Peterson how it was done, sending my Omega paralight Deathcraft through a gravitational wormhole into alien space, where I quickly found a nest and proceeded to wipe it out. I swiftly collected points against a backdrop of intricately woven explosions, shattering rocks, dying monsters with their insides erupting, and tangled burning alien machinery.

Wipeout took me five minutes. I earned three battle-pips, a free play, and the adulation of the handful of kids who'd stood round watching me do it.

"So." I swiped my sweating palms on my jeans and stood back from the joystick controls. "Whatcha think, Peterson?"

He considered it for a few moments, frowning hard, then he said, "Well, it's a bit sad, really."

"What!" I felt ready to deck him.

"Well, all of those alien species look monstrous, and all of them want to destroy us. I just can't believe things would actually be like that." He looked up at me. "Do you?"

Instead of bothering to answer him, I told him which button to push to play, then I went off to have a Coke.

*   *   *   *   *

To give him his due, Peterson stayed with it for a week or so, chalking up a respectable 50,000 score on the Basement Level of the easiest mission. Not to boast or anything, but by the same time I'd achieved over a hundred-thou on Rooftop Level of a middle-difficulty campaign, a mission called Rock And A Hard Place. Made me chuckle, really, being so much like life.

After ten days or so, Ben and I had 'buddied-up' about as much as we were going to. He was coming to Gemini more regularly (as I was - the machines still had plenty of play value in them!), and we bought each other colas and things, and sat and talked; but then Ben would take himself off for a game of pool or table tennis with some of the other kids. That was OK. Sellers saw that I'd been doing my bit and that Ben was settling well and putting down little roots into the social soil of the centre.

"I'm pleased with you, Steve, pleased and proud," Sellers said one time, sitting beside me as I took a break from saving the entire cosmos. "You haven't patronised Ben, you haven't been cool towards him - "

"I'm always cool, Mr Sellers," I pointed out coolly, and we both laughed at my little joke.

"You know what I mean." His smile warmed. "Here, you deserve this..."

He held out ten pound coins. I looked at them but didn't take them.

"For the machines," he added. I shrugged, oiled and easy.

"Don't need it. I've racked up twenty free plays on Alien Berserker already. That will be fifty plays by next week. So, thanks anyway - but you were the one who was talking about responsibility. I'm being responsible for myself now..."

"That's fine," Sellers said, nodding. "That's just fine, Steve."

He gripped my shoulder as he stood up, and it pleased me to think that Sellers felt he'd succeeded in some kind of mission too.

The next evening I turned up and got a shock. The display screen was glowing with the Alien Berserker panel showing the five most recent highscores - with mine in second place, behind some kid called Brag. What was most amazing was that he had topped my best by a clear five-K, taking him past the 150,000 point mark.

I scowled and looked around at the half dozen or so kids in the centre this early on; two playing pool, a couple over at the drinks vendor sorting coinage, and two others reading magazines across the way.

"Hey - any of you lot go by the nickname of Brag?"

"Nope," one boy bothered to say. The others shook their heads lethargically.

"Any of you know who Brag is?"

I might as well have been talking to a bag of potatoes, so I turned back and decided to give my anonymous rival a beating. I keyed-in my code word and the screen swirled in a storm of rainbow pixels, the synthsound kicking in dramatically...

On thousands of worlds among the millions of stars scattered through the boundless universe, the eternal battle of light against dark continues...

The game title, Alien Berserker, appeared in 3–D granite effect, letters of rock the size of cliff-faces. Then they shattered into a panorama of endless deep space and I was cruising.

I picked my ship, loaded up with nova-bombs and dark matter pulse cannon, set my course and went out to kick alien ass.

Twenty minutes later, my hands throbbing sore and my face covered with sweat, I edged past Brag's one-fifty K and made it to one-sixty before being slimed by an Emperor Alien who'd snuck up behind me on Theta Aurigae Six...

But I'd done it, pulled myself up to pole position again - top-gunned this kid Brag right out of the sky.

I went and treated myself to a can; bought one for Ben, too, when he came in later. We chatted about this and that, about the long humid spell of weather that was all set to break soon; about our plans for the rest of the summer holiday; about how the Gemini Centre wasn't so bad after all; and about my triumphant gameplaying.

As I gave Ben the jaw about my excellent work, a thought occurred to me. I frowned at him, pausing.

"Ben...I don't suppose you could be..." Then I grinned at the look on his face.

"Just forget it. It's impossible."

We stayed on till late, made a nodding hello to Mr Sellers who breezed through to speak with Don Harris, the regular 'adult presence' at Gemini, and left around ten, just as the storm was breaking.

The quickest way home for both Ben and me was across the wasteground and on to the estate. It was an old factory lot that had been empty for some years, waiting for redevelopment. The building itself had been bulldozed; all there was now amounted to little hills of bricks and rubble and flat expanses of cracked concrete sprouting wild weeds and bushes. We usually sneaked in through a hole in the chain-link, cutting five minutes' walk from our journey...But tonight we didn't bother. Neither Ben nor I said anything, but I could see he was as unnerved as I was. Something about the wasteland wasn't right...And when you looked at it, it was as though your eyes were not able to see it properly...Not able to see what was really there...

I put it out of my mind after that, turned in and tried to sleep.

The storm kept me awake. The storm, and wondering who Brag might be, and how he could just wander in to the centre, top my best, and then vanish without trumpeting his victory. Didn't make sense.

By midnight I was still tossing and turning, so went to my window to watch the lightning. It was spectacular over the city... And for long moments I failed to notice the fainter flickering light closer to, just beyond the empty lot - inside the Gemini Centre. When I did spot it, I thought the electrics might be shorting out, or something. But then I realised with a jolt it was the flare and glow of the games machines. Someone was in there playing them -

And I thought I knew just who it would be.

*   *   *   *   *

The kid obviously just couldn't care less. Either that, or he was stupid. He'd left the door to the centre wide open and swinging in the wind. The place was in darkness, only one machine was active, and by its light I watched Brag play...

He was good. He was very good. Alien Berserker used a joystick and a six-button keypad to the left of it. You could use either or both on the mission. Brag was using both. His right hand was wrapped around the joystick, while the fingers of his left fluttered on the keys. Those fingers seemed boneless, and moved almost too fast for me to follow. He was hunched over the game, his big squarish head hung low as he moved his ship across the world called Ultima Thule with exquisite ease, but remorselessly, as though he wasn't enjoying it at all but was doing it to prove something important.

I edged closer, stopping a couple of yards away. I didn't like the look of Brag, and I didn't like his smell either. It was hard to describe, an animal kind of smell, nauseating and unnatural. Part of me wanted to turn and run away - a big part! But a proud voice inside was telling me to stay put and see this through...

So I waited until, inevitably, Brag's last game-life was lost against the rocks of Ultima Thule. I jumped as he gave a guttural groan of frustration, then stepped back from the screen, his square dwarfish body held rigid with anger.

Perhaps I made some sound then, a shoe scuffed on the floor. Brag turned with a look, not of startlement, but of expectation.

And he laughed, a dry and thickish sound as though his mouth was packed with dirt: it yawned open, and inside his tongue was white and bloodless.

He stood, allowing me to play - something I hardly wanted to do right then. The guy scared me, I admit it; the shape of him, the weird pallor of his skin, his too-large eyes with that expression of sly curiosity in them...

It would be easy to have panicked, lost concentration, and made a fatal error. I kept it cool, though, choosing not the most powerful ship in the fleet, but the one I was most familiar with. I stocked up with my favourite weapons, nova-bombs and pulse cannon, and headed straight for the heart of alien territory.

Over the next thirty minutes, the campaign went smoothly, but I wasn't clocking up the points I needed. I kept myself locked on the task, shutting Brag out as best I could. I could feel him beside me, though; could smell his foul mouth and hear the deep raggedness of his slow breathing. He was willing me to lose it, to come apart and end up as space dust...

Outside, the lightnings jabbed at the city and the thunder growled overhead, like a booming backdrop to the snap and sizzle of my own weaponry and the little detonations of alien ships exploding.

There came a point, over half an hour into the game, when I felt things slipping away from me. My hand was slick on the joystick, and my back and neck muscles burned. Over the long minutes, Brag had eased closer, until now he was touching me, shoulder to shoulder. I wanted to yell at him, wanted to land my best right hand jab smack bang on his flat and shapeless nose. I wanted to pulp him, like I had pulped these hundreds of aliens swarming on the screen... I wanted - I wanted -

He was doing it to my mind; putting on this pressure to trip me. I felt him in my head, moving spiderlike among my thoughts. He had hold of me now and if he took me, then not just me, but my kind would have lost face in defeat.

I felt on the edge - and then the alien Supercruiser hove into view in a hurricane of light. I dodged a crossflash of lasers, swung to firing position in a second and stab-stabbed the fire button on the joystick.

The first dark matter pulse missed, the second hit target dead centre.

The Supercruiser seemed to hold itself together momentarily, then erupted in a starburst of brilliance and glimmering sparks, slowly fading...

My highscore tumbled upward, past Brag's 160K, and I let it go at that, not bothering to battle beyond it...

I clenched my fist and held it up in front of Brag. Briefly he looked as though his vast mouth was going to open and bite my hand off at the wrist...But he knew when he was beaten, fair and square. He said nothing, but with a throaty snarl turned and shambled to the door, slammed his way through and disappeared into the might. And it occurred to me then that Brag must have come from somewhere terribly dark and terribly cold; and I was glad I had beaten him, because he didn't belong here at all.

It doesn't shame me to say that I didn't follow him out for over ten minutes. When I did leave eventually, I switched off the machine and closed the door of the centre behind me. No-one need know what had happened - even if they'd believe it in the first place.

I skirted the wasteland homewards, even though it looked normal again now. And I slept in late next day, telling my Mum that saving the world was hard work, and I reckoned I wouldn't be rising till noon.

*   *   *   *   *

Nanoman

There was something weird about him, that was for sure. He was too calm. Too composed. In his place, Skat would have been suffering a full sweat knowing that if the General caught up with him, he'd order the troops to fire on sight - summary execution for an enemy of the State.

"So whatcha called, pilgrim?" She cast a glance at the stranger's eyes, and looked away again quickly. Skat figured she was a good judge of character; had to be in her line of work, on the streets, finding rat-runs for people to escape from the Zone (and sometimes even the planet, as in this case). But his face was a closed book: handsome, fresh, twenty-something, and totally unreadable.

"My name is John."

"John?"

The Medic giggled. "John Doe. Y'know Skat, the tag the Kops give to dead bodies they can't identify. At least he's got a sense of humour. And he'll need one...We all will..."

The Medic's smile faded a little as he thought of the challenge before them: acquire a fast-bolt vehicle, hit the launchport running and smuggle John Doe aboard an outgoing freight ship bound for deep space. Beyond the General's reach. Maybe.

They were sitting around a battered moulded-plastic table in a seedy coffee house downZone; Skat, who would deal with the sharp end of the business; the Medic, making people's lives better. He had arranged the links in the escape chain. And Silent Blade, the computer phreak. So called because he could hack into virtually any system without a soul knowing. He would be worth his weight in silicon superchips later, when the time came to slip through the electronic security fences at the launchport and alter the freight ship's weight log. They all knew that the only way to keep John Doe alive would be to make him computer-invisible. He could only continue to exist if, as far as the Zone computer, Little Sister, was concerned, he had ceased to exist.

"So." Skat hid her unease by staring the Medic in the face and speaking briskly.

"What do I need to know?"

"What do you know already?"

"Only what Blade here has told me, that our customer is top man in the field of nanotechnology - the science of the super small. But how small? Grains of sand sized?"

"Not quite," John said in the easy going way that was beginning to irritate Skat intensely.

"Look out there." He pointed through the steamed up rain-streaked window to one of the towerblocks reaching into the underbelly of low grey cloud. "Imagine that 'scraper is only a millimetre in height –"

"So we would be the size of nanomachines, yeah?" The Medic sounded impressed.

John shook his head slowly.

"No. These would be the size of nanomachines."

He upended a salt dispenser and scattered white crystals over the table.

"They are properly called nanocules," John said. "Self-sufficient machines that can be designed to perform any number of functions. Imagine a nanocule army inside a human body, repairing damage, fighting bacteria and viruses more efficiently than the body's own systems. People might double or treble their life spans..."

"And if they were in computers?"

The others looked at Silent Blade. Tall, blonde, hard as granite; he rarely spoke and showed emotion even less often. But now he sounded almost excited.

John Doe shrugged with a strange rippling of his shoulders that added to Skat's uneasy impression of him.

"In the early days they would scan and repair hard drives in microseconds. But soon after that, nanocules would be computers themselves, encoding information by rearranging individual atoms. Everybody could have all the world's knowledge inside their head."

"Which is why the General wants you silenced." Skat drew in a slow breath. "The secrets you carry would mean an end to the Zone. The death of Little Sister."

John nodded. "People would be free at last. It's not a question of whether or not nanocules could make a difference. Once they are released, change would be inevitable."

Skat held out her hand. And smiled.

"Then welcome to the Good Fight, John," she said quietly.

*   *   *   *   *

The Zone. A megacity measuring over ten million square kilometres from rim to rim: larger than Brazil, it stretched from Morocco to Iceland, and eastward deep into the scattered splinter states of the old Soviet bloc. Hundreds of sub-Atlantic freightway tunnels connected the Zone to the Amerikas, but right from the outset Skat knew this would be a dangerous route to take. Although there was heavy continuous traffic through the system, everything was carefully checked both ways by battalions of Zone Kops. Nothing could slip through their net. And they shot anyone who looked at all suspicious.

Perhaps, Skat thought as the group left the coffee house and took to the streets, perhaps John could have continued his work within the Zone itself. He had told them he needed just a few months more to perfect the nanocule driveware. At the moment the nanocules he had developed were not fully co-ordinated. They were like a poorly drilled regiment, not completely within the control of the main unit.

"One day," John had said, "nanocule clusters will be independent. They'll make up their own minds about things. But for now they need to be guided - like a queen ant controlling her nest."

"And just where is the nanocules' 'queen ant' right now?" the Medic had asked.

John tapped the side of his head. "That's for me to know and you to wonder about. Safer that way."

And the Medic, to Skat's surprise, had not argued.

There were six billion people living in the Zone. Most of them were registered on Little Sister's database. But there were millions who, for one reason or another, did not have an official identity. Skat liked things that way. As an N.P - non-person - you could move freely through the city, only getting into trouble if the Kops bothered to stop you, or if you were spotted by a surveillance system programmed to look out for your profile. Silent Blade preferred a false I.D., because that allowed him to access computer systems, make money transactions, and conduct all the other business of an electronic age. But in that respect, Blade was the weak point in the plan: whenever he plugged-in to the electric life of the Zone, he could be traced.

Skat knew the streets and alleys of this part of down Zone like her own face. She led the group through the endless thin drizzle and the bustling, shuffling crowds, taking a tortuous route in the market quarter that would reduce their chances of detection. And she played it cool, telling the others to pretend they were browsing from time to time, lingering over this stall or that, as though to buy.

"You're a calm customer," John told her. They were standing together at a jewellery stall, Skat scanning through the trays of rings and rows of silver necklaces. His words were accompanied by the musical tinkling of metal as the trinkets moved in the breeze. "I expected you to be like the other people who've helped me - nervous, frightened. But you're not. I like your style."

Skat was flattered by the comment, but withheld her smile. "Oh, don't overestimate me. I'm frightened all right. You know that any action against the State is punishable by death. The point is, this is good camouflage. The spycams are monitored to react to people acting suspiciously: you panic, and all the alarms go off..."

She picked out a thin chain hung with a raindrop of amethyst and held it up to her collarbones, gazing at herself critically in the mirror.

"How old are you, Skat?" John wondered. Coming from him, it did not sound like a personal question.

"Fifteen," she said, knowing that her black hair, cut as short as it was, made her look older. John shook his head.

"I've been hiding for over half of your life. How - um..."

He grew embarrassed then, thinking he was intruding.

"How did I end up like this? I only ever knew my Mom," Skat said. Her gaze in the glass had become fixed now. "She was in the Resistance too. Good with words. She used to challenge Government policy by putting articles out on the Web. Who was it once said that words are loaded pistols? Well, she blew a few holes in Little Sister's arguments before they caught up with her..."

"I see."

Skat put the necklace back on its hook.

"There was some warning. Friends smuggled me away before Mom was taken. I've been carrying on her work ever since, though in a different way. Who knows, maybe she's alive somewhere."

A hot tightness clenched in Skat's throat. She looked away and saw the Medic moving purposefully towards them.

"Stay cool," he said, tilting his head so his spectacles flashed back streetlight.

"The Kops are about."

Skat glanced over his shoulder at the unit of three Zone Kops pushing their way through the crowds. They were in full armour; bulky, dull grey, looking more like heavy-duty machines than human beings. They carried stubby a.p.r's – all-purpose rifles - but their bronze armbands told Skat they were only on routine patrol.

"Let's tough it out," Skat advised, turning back to the stall as the Kops shouldered by within an arm's reach. So close that she could hear the radio conversation between the officers and Divisional Control going on inside the ugly full-face helmets.

The Kops moved off and the Medic let out a tense breath. "This is not good for my health!"

"Getting caught would be worse," Blade reminded him. "Come on. Let's go."

Skat began to move. John held her arm gently and pressed something into her hand. The silver-and-amethyst necklace.

"A token," he said, "for help I can never repay."

It was the first gift she'd received since her mother had left.

＊　　＊　　＊　　＊　　＊

They reached the recycle yard by evening. A glorious fresh evening, purple sky filled with fiery red clouds.

The yard was a vast enclosure where the worn out products of civilisation were repaired and put back to use; everything from wristwatches to moon hoppers. Anyone could buy or part-trade recycled items, and even at this late hour 'scrap city' was bustling.

The Medic had contacts here, people who would do him some special deals. So once the group was inside the yard, it was the Medic who took over, leading his friends away from the brightly floodlit main avenues, down dimmer sideways to a small black hangar. A man in work overalls was sitting in a rocking chair made from chrome-plated tubular steel. He was whistling softly to himself as he watched the stars come out.

"Hi there Hammer," the Medic called out cheerfully. "How's the nuts and bolts business?"

"Couldn't be better, friend." Hammer stood up and nodded to the Medic's companions. He was tall and gangly thin, his hair tied back in a stringy ponytail.

"You got the money?"

"You got the goods?"

They grinned at one another, each producing a small plastic transaction card.

"Four K, like we agreed?" the Medic said. Hammer nodded, offering up his card. The Medic did the same. The cards kissed, and the credit was transferred.

"You've got yourselves a bargain." Hammer slid back the hangar doors to reveal the bolt-vehicle the group would ride to the launchport. It was a scarab, squat, black and murderous-looking, like some alien bug bristling with sensors. A tiny green-blue eye, the standby light, winked at them in a steady rhythm above the hatchway. On-off. On-off.

"It's ex-military," Hammer pointed out. "No weapons. I had to strip those out. But the engines and guidance systems are standard. It'll take you half-way around the world in under an hour."

"Good enough." The Medic stepped into the hangar and walked around the ship.

"Forward and prime for launch!"

Instantly the scarab obeyed, rolling smoothly forward on its half-tracks. More lights blinked on in clusters while systems came online. And there was a rising whine as the engines powered up.

"It's radar-silent," Hammer said, grinning his wide white salesman's grin. "A feature I offer you at no extra cost."

"I should think not." The Medic grinned back. "I've done you enough favours in the past, good buddy."

The scarab came to rest just metres from the group, the hatch sliding silently open. Its matt black surface reflected no light. Skat thought it looked as though it could do the job. But in the past she'd found that appearances could be deceptive, and wondered now if the ship would live up to its promise.

"OK Blade - in first, and check out the networks, please."

"Ma'am." The Blade hopped aboard. Skat glanced at John and offered a reassuring smile.

"...if you use tight-beam trajectory mapping, you can home right in to the beacon at the Coast East launchport – " Hammer was saying. He stopped abruptly, looking confused.

"Flight time?" the Medic asked. But his friend's eyes were fixed and glassy.

"Hammer?"

A blue point of light appeared in the centre of Hammer's eyes; a light that swiftly and suddenly spread outwards in a spiderweb of thin strands, trickling up over his head, flowing down to envelop his entire body. The man began to shudder. A faint crackling sound filled the air.

"Volt-net!" Skat yelled. "Into the ship - now!"

Her words seemed to trigger more trouble. As Hammer folded to the ground unconscious, a tightly-wrapped ball of glowing blue light just missed the Medic and smacked into the side of the scarab, where it spat and buzzed and harmlessly dissolved. Volt-net, a Kop weapon, designed to capture not kill. But it was accompanied by rapid bursts of a.p.r. fire which chewed up the dust close to where Skat was standing. Somehow the Zone Kops had found out about the meet; were intending to take John alive and wipe out the rest of them.

Even as the thought flashed across Skat's mind, a dozen Kops in full armour lumbered into view. Blackbands. A kill squad. Just behind them dust was billowing as a tank-like personnel carrier swung round the hills of metal scrap. Instantly its guns opened up, filling the air with bullets and energy beams and zipping points of tracer light.

There came a sigh of power restrained. The scarab lifted half a body height off the ground and hung there, bouncing gently on its drive fields. Blade's head appeared out of the hatchway.

"Time to leave, people – "

Skat grabbed John's arm and began to pull him to safety. He had just been standing, as though mesmerised.

The Medic dropped to one knee, snapped a pulsegun from his belt clip and returned some covering fire.

"We - were - betrayed..." John's voice was incredulous. "But who?"

"Maybe Hammer," Skat said. "Who knows. Let's just get out of here – "

Her words were cut off by a loud thud and a bloom of brilliant light. A dazzling spray of shrapnel exploded outwards and came spinning towards them. Fragments tinkled against the scarab and piles of nearby scrap: Skat felt one piece touch her temple as it flew by, scalding her skin. The Medic was not so lucky. There was a wet slap and he was flung backwards, blood spreading over his tunic.

"No!" Skat screamed in rage and loss.

"Leave him," Blade called. "He's dead. Get aboard!"

Skat felt as if she was in a storm of grief and pain. They would all be killed in seconds and the mission failed. The Kops were just twenty metres away, their gunfire deafening.

Then, like a quiet moment in the eye of the hurricane, John was there, as calm as Skat should have been.

"Take your friend into the ship. I'll join you in a moment."

There was something in his voice - a gentle power - that made Skat obey instantly. She took hold of the Medic's body under his arms and hauled him to the ship. Blade grabbed his coat collar and dragged him inside.

Skat turned to help John. He was a few metres away, wrapped in a milky cloud. Tendrils of the cloud were spreading outwards, wafting over the Kops and the grinding bulk of the vehicle behind them.

And Skat was astonished to see that the Kops were falling like clockwork robots, their springs unwound. The cloud of - whatever it was - streamed over and left them lying. Then it attacked the personnel carrier, eating into the high-tensile metal and ceramic as though it was meringue; crumbling it away into rusty powder.

84

The front end of the carrier dropped forward as its fore-axles disintegrated. It nosedived into the dirt with a roaring of over-revving engines. Black smoke and sparks gushed from its exhaust vents as the engines themselves broke down and came apart; followed by the scream of steel spinning on steel; then a flash and the dull boom of an explosion inside. The carrier lay still, disabled and helpless like a felled stegosaurus.

Skat stood amazed, not just at this: John seemed to breathe the cloud back in, drawing it down into himself in just a few seconds, leaving all around him the scattered remnants of the Kops' attack.

But in the distance, sweeping down out of the sunset, other Kop ships were approaching. Too many to fight. John spotted them and hurried with Skat into the scarab.

*   *   *   *   *

They cruised the stratosphere on a high, wide, sub-orbital curve. Outside the sky was black and crystalline, filled with glittering pinpoints - the city and the stars.

All of the group was gathered around the Medic. He had been badly wounded. A chest shot. His breathing was ragged and raw.

"He's dying," Skat said, trying to hold in a sob. They'd used the onboard autodoc to try to limit the bleeding, but the wound was too deep and too complex. Skat had never felt so helpless.

"What you did, John, back at scrap city..." Blade's voice was low and cautious.

"Can you work the same magic now - or better? Can you put together as well as just take apart?"

John smiled the first smile Skat had seen from him.

"I think I might be able to help. Give me a moment..."

They stood aside and watched as John hunched low over the Medic, as though listening hard. His face was very pale now, his breathing shallow and weak. Skat could all but see the life force trickling out of him to leave his body empty and abandoned.

"Yes," John whispered moments later. "They can do it..."

A thin smoke began drifting from his fingers: like dry ice it sank down and enfolded the Medic, wrapping him in fog so that his form grew indistinct and milky.

"These are your nanomachines – " It was as though Skat had just realised the marvel. "So small, like powder."

"Different nanocules are designed to do different jobs. The ones I've deployed maintain life support functions. They can repair destroyed cells, minimise shock, rebuild bone and flesh..."

Skat had no doubt this was true. Already, within a minute, the Medic's breathing sounded stronger and healthier. He shuddered and let out a groan. The pearly nanocule-mist began to withdraw, back into John's body.

"You keep them inside yourself - all those millions of machines!"

"It's like having a house full of friends." John chuckled. Then his smile mellowed, became serious. "To add to the three I've made today."

The Medic's recovery was swift and sure. Within a few minutes he opened his eyes and looked blearily up at the others.

"Ooohhh...Where am I?"

"In the scarab," Blade said, clearly delighted. "It's not home, but it's better than where you were headed – "

A chime sounded politely in the chamber.

'Attention. Attack formation detected. Fifty kilometres northeast and closing. Suggest evasive action.'

The soft, gentle, synthetic female voice of the ship's computer filled them with dread.

"They're on to us. Strap in. This will be rough – "

No sooner had Skat spoken than the ship was buffetted as though by a huge wave. A wash of angry red light splashed across the forward viewports. There was a blue flash and showers of sparks as systems short-circuited. Boards blew, and the cabin filled with an acrid smoke. Alarms chirruped shrilly. Monitor lights blinked red.

"I'm going to manual control!" Skat yelled above the din. "They'll wipe us off the sky unless we ditch!"

Another percussion bomb impacted on the hull. The scarab canted right. Its blunt nose dropped alarmingly. Skat was hurled forward and grabbed the pilot's chair-back, so saving herself from being injured. In the background, almost inaudible, the computer voice was reporting disaster: main control and navigation systems gone; hull integrity breached; multiple fires burning vigorously behind the inner bulkhead. The scarab was turning swiftly into a fireball as it tumbled from the sky.

"We'll have to abort mission!" Blade grabbed Skat's arm and dragged her round to face him. "Now!"

"But what about John - he has to get away."

"If he stays he'll go down in flames like the ship!"

"Blade's right." John came forward and handed Skat an eject pack. "There's no way we'll reach the launchport now."

"If I can guide her in we'll have a chance – "

"You're talking dreams, girl." Blade buckled his own

pack about him. The Medic was already waiting by the exit hatch. "Let's do it by the book. I'll team with Medic. You stay with John. We'll get back to the city and rendezvous at the usual place - say, five days from now?"

Skat nodded grimly.

"Safe home," Blade said. He pointed at the Medic, who hit the door release switch. Two explosive bolts flung the hatch into space. A howling, frigid wind swept through the cabin. The Medic was gone, whirled into the sky. Blade followed a moment later.

Together Skat and John struggled toward the hatch. Outside, the freezing black heavens were filled with spinning stars, some of them moving smoothly in for the kill.

"Put your eject pack on!" Skat screamed. John gave a little shrug of his shoulders.

"There were only three! Maybe Hammer did betray us after all - who knows!"

"But John – "

"It's not important. We'll both survive. But only if you help me, Skat. What I'm about to tell you is my deepest secret. And your most profound responsibility..."

Quickly he explained what he meant. Skat listened intently. And the end of it she realised why the General wanted John destroyed. Because if he lived, the world would never be the same again.

When he had finished, John knew by Skat's eyes that she had agreed.

"What do I have to do?" she wondered.

"Just hold my hand. Don't be afraid. I'm with you."

She did as she was told. But even as John's fingers gripped hers, his flesh was evaporating, rendering down into the milky smoke she had seen before.

The miracle happened quickly, giving Skat time enough to jump ship at several hundred metres and watch it whirl down to earth. The scarab plunged into a mountain lake, one of the wilderness enclaves dotted about the Zone. It exploded in the depths and filled the waters with a brief white glow.

Even if it was not totally destroyed, the drag-teams would find precious little of John's remains aboard; some robotics, a simple carbonite skeleton. The rest of him travelled with her, a part of her, like an unborn child. But more than that. A protector and companion. For he was in her eyes and in her seeing: in her head, and in her understanding.

Skat landed safely near the northern fringe of the wild ground. Overhead the Kop ships were searching, a crisscross sweep pattern. But Skat was safe. They would not find her now.

Down in the valley a million streets lay waiting. Their shadows welcomed Skat home. Maybe in the weeks and months that followed she and Blade and the Medic would try again, successfully, to realise John's grand dream. But for now she would just keep running.

It was what she did best.

※　　※　　※　　※　　※

The House that R'ork Built

"This it?" I wondered. Jeff nodded. His eyes were alight.

"It is the focal point, Louis. Can't you feel the lines of power converging here?"

I cocked a thumb at the pylons striding away over the fields and into the evening distance.

"Yeah, and hear them..." The wires were humming gently.

"Lines of power, you idiot, not power lines."

Jeff grinned. He was used to my sarcasm - never meant harmfully - and always forgave it.

Well, I was the only person we both knew who'd tolerate Jeff's UFO mania. He'd been seeing aliens up every side alley since kindergarten, and writing about them, and joining clubs filled with other freaks and loners. Maybe it had started out as simple curiosity, a taste for the 'sense of wonder' he was always talking about. Maybe. But now it was his life, and I at least knew that he could never pull himself out of it. Jeff Collis had given up real life for ever and committed himself to his dream.

"It's there, centered in that house..."

Jeff pointed through purple September gloom to the big square shadow of a house set alone in a half-circling of trees a hundred yards from the road. I thought it was where Glebe House had once stood, but that place was no more than a broken shell: this house was complete, lived in too. A single light shone from a downstairs window.

I looked up and down the road for Glebe, but there was nothing; fields, a copse, the glitter of Raybrooke over a mile away, a nearby telephone box.

"Must be the wrong place."

"What?"

"I said, they must have come from outer space."

"Who?"

"The family living in that big old house. Well, it's cheaper than the Holiday Inn."

Jeff chuckled, but emptily. I knew that his humour was being replaced by the cosmic seriousness that usually infected him on a saucer-trek.

"Maybe they've parked their starship round back."

"Come on," Jeff said, "let's investigate."

The truth was that I was nervous - not of a CE3K (Close Encounter of the Third Kind) you understand - but of making a total fool of myself in front of whoever we came across in our hunt for intergalactic beings. I had suffered my worst embarrassments in the company of Jeff Collis, and once almost had a backside full of buckshot when we were caught trespassing on private ground.

But none of that ever made any difference to Jeff. He had stars in his eyes and took no notice of trivialities like the law and mortal danger.

We crossed the road and leant on the gate that barred the long driveway up to the house.

"How do you know you're going to find something, Jeff?"

"It's nearly nine o'clock and it's Wednesday."

"Ah yes, that explains it all."

"It's in the BUFOD guide - the Bureau for UFO Detection, page eighty-two actually."

"Nine p.m. Wednesdays is when the aliens come out to play...?"

"No Louis." Jeff's voice held a tone of carefully, and barely, controlled patience.

"Statistically, most UFOs are seen between nine in the evening and midnight. Also, Wednesday is the most popular day for sightings, and the twenty-fourth of the month is very significant in UFO lore."

I said, "I thought you were taking the scientific approach."

"Sure, but Man is a subtle mixture of the rational and the instinctive, just as the universe is a blending of the logical and unexplainable. I use my whole self in these investigations."

"Sorry I asked. But I'll tell you something mysterious..."

"Hm?" Jeff was busy making notes in his little UFO spotter's book. I pointed at the driveway.

"No-one's been along here all week, or maybe longer. No tyre marks in the soft mud, and the grass growing in the ruts is upright and undisturbed."

"Score one for you, Louis." Jeff smiled and clambered over the gate. What could I do but follow?

"They probably arrived by matter transmitter," he said.

One thing that I constantly admire about Jeff is his determination, both to boldly go where no man has gone before, and to maintain his dignity while spouting the most ridiculous rubbish. You can never bait him: he'll never lose his temper or back down from holding his absurd beliefs.

And he wasn't kidding with the matter transmitter idea. "Maybe we could just do a very general interview with the people living here," I said. Jeff was two steps ahead, striding squelchily along the ridge between the ruts.

"I mean, say it's for our school magazine or something."

"We'll take it as it comes. I've got the tape recorder ready, and the lump of iron."

"Oh?"

"It repels any creature of a vampiric or lycanthropic nature."

"Well thank God you remembered the lump of iron, Jeff."

"I knew you'd appreciate my foresight..."

He was deep into the mad-professor role now, so my function had to change from a vaguely interested and mildly sceptical disciple to a guardian and negotiator who would try to prevent these innocent country folk from calling the police and having him taken away...

We reached the gravel sweep in front of the house, but instead of knocking politely at the door, Jeff decided to 'scout round the back' for clues.

"For goodness' sake! Maybe they've got dogs - big ones, Jeff, with teeth. You know teeth - they chew legs off."

"Alien infiltrators would not risk detection by causing the disappearance of two local and well known boys. They would be more sophisticated – "

"Replace us with independently conscious holograms until their plan for world domination reached fruition."

Jeff stopped dead and swung around to face me, his expression one of deep suspicion, one almost of fear.

"Have you been reading my secret notebooks - because that's how I think they'll do it...."

He was serious! So I kept the smirk off my face and just shrugged.

"Great minds, Jeff, that's all. Or maybe we're telepathetic."

"Telepathic."

"I know what I mean."

"Well," Jeff said, "at last you're thinking along the right lines. You ought to join BUFOD, you know. We're always on the lookout for sharp new minds."

"Do I get a badge?"

"Anyway, if dogs were around they'd've sensed us by this time and set up a row." He paused significantly. "Come to think of it, I can't hear any animals."

That at least was a fact. Apart from the cool soughing of the wind in the dark pines, the world was silent: no dogs, cats, birds, traffic or poltergeists. Jeff made more notes in his book. I stared thoughtfully back the way we'd come.

"Actually Jeff, there is a kind of atmosphere here. I'm not usually sensitive to them, but I'll admit something's in the air - and it's not the smell of cows..."

I turned round for him to appreciate my wit, but he was already at the door, and it was open, and a warm rectangle of gold light cast Jeff in silhouette: lanky, stooped, with a haloed mop of curly, infrequently-cut hair. He was staring at the figure of a man who had silently appeared.

If I'd had any sense, I would have set off home at a run and not looked back.

I wandered over with a big stupid smile on my face.

"Look," I began to the man at the door, "I hope you don't mind. We're doing this research for our school magazine and – "

And I almost wet myself. Jeff was just staring in silence at the same thing.

The man was like a badly molded lump of clay. That was my first snapshot impression. My second was a readjustment of the senses coupled with a feeling of guilt and shame that I should think so cruelly of someone disabled.

It was as though he could not stand upright, without the support of the wall. He was leaning weakly against it, his pale right hand pressed hard against what looked like bare pink plaster. His body was skeletal, the thin covering of flesh over the bones seeming white and bloodless.

The man's hair was lifeless grey. His eyes were empty.

There was more than that. The house itself. Even as I thought it, a second inner voice told me severely that I was beginning to believe the same meaningless nonsense as Jeff.

But it was there, a vivid sense that the house was more alive than its occupant. The air was warm, rich with the smells of life - like a barn, but elusively different. And it was thickly heavy, greenhouse air, so dense that it very nearly shimmered.

"Perhaps," I said to Jeff, my voice quavering and quiet, "perhaps we should not disturb the gentleman. It is quite late, you know - on this Wednesday, the twenty-fourth... "

"No, he's just what we want."

I saw Jeff jab a finger to the side of the canvas bag that was slung over his shoulder; he'd set his tape recorder running, and the interview had started whether I liked it or not.

The man's mouth opened. Inside it was white and the pale tongue lay still like a dead fish on a bare sea-bed.

"Pl-ease co-me in."

I wasn't sure if the man's accent was thickly foreign, or if the words themselves were so badly slurred as to be almost indecipherable. But what surprised me most was that the sound seemed to come from the walls and ceiling, a great blow of sound, a huge exaggeration of a man-sized voice.

Even Jeff took a step back, but as his silly impulsive legs walked him over the threshold, he turned his head and gave me a chuckling look.

"We've cracked it Louis. This is the one, man!"

"Something's cracked you, more like," I snapped, unnerved but not surprised when my impulsive legs carried me after him...

The house was rather bare, drab, unbearably stuffy - and odd. I felt the elusive strangeness of the place from the first moment. It scared me. The feeling reminded me of what a mouse might experience as it put a tentative paw on the wooden platform where the cheese lay. At any second I expected a monster to leap out in front of me or sneak up behind me. Thank God for Jeff's lump of iron.

We followed the man along a corridor towards a room off to the right. Another thing bothered me: he never took his hand away from the wall. And, as the palm passed across, the plaster seemed to ripple like blancmange that had not quite set. Curious, I touched the wall myself, and the damn thing was warm! Underfloor heating I'd heard of, but this was ridiculous.

The man took us into the room and indicated some brownish armchairs opposite the door.

"Do - sit," he said, just about.

"Thanks." Jeff was visibly shaking with excitement, though I couldn't understand why. My shaking was of a different variety, because I was starting to have thoughts about kidnappers and psychopaths and vampires. The image kind of crawled out from under a wall of carefully cultivated disbelief and conventional education. Vampires didn't exist, so this weirdo couldn't be one. QED, right?

But I was still scared.

I sat in one armchair, Jeff in another. The material of the furniture seemed to be a sort of plastic that was slightly tacky to the touch; it was vaguely repellent. And for a few seconds it disorientated me, because I could have sworn the chair shifted the substance of itself to accommodate my exact shape.

Jeff started too. The man slowly lowered himself on to the sofa nearby, only releasing his contact with the wall when he was fully seated.

"Now then," Jeff began, notebook in hand. "Let's not beat around the bush. I have reason to suspect that you are not what you appear, Mr – "

"R'ork," came the reply, a frog's croak of a word.

"Mr R'ork. In fact, I strongly suspect that you are a being from another world, quite possibly from a planet beyond our galaxy."

Jeff beamed amiably, though his eyes were sharp and alert with anticipation. I could have curled up and died. However odd this R'ork person was, we must have seemed to be one egg short of a dozen, you know what I mean...

As it turned out, the situation did not develop as I expected. R'ork sat very still for perhaps a minute, then nodded gravely and returned Jeff's smile - that is, if the twisted travesty of an expression his lips made could be called a smile.

"You hum-ans are very sh-rewd. I th-ought my cam-ouflage was complete."

"So you admit it!"

"I ad-mit it."

I couldn't believe what I was hearing! My mental alarm jumped up a number of notches as I realised that I was surrounded by loonies – me, the only sane individual for miles around. And I suddenly had doubts about myself -

The wall clock over the fireplace was melting.

"You must for-give me," R'ork continued shakily. "It is ha-ard for me to communicate in th-is form."

Jeff cast a triumphant glance my way: after years of humiliation and even persecution he was being proved right. All his dreams were coming true, and he smiled, even as R'ork began to disintegrate from something just about bearably human to something utterly and completely alien.

His body swiftly sank into the substance of the sofa, losing detail and colour, becoming plastic like a candle in an oven. The viscous movement of it was a little like a deflating balloon, a little like thick syrup overflowing from its jar. It was disgusting but, at the same time, fascinating. I sat transfixed for maybe two, three minutes while it happened, before I noticed something else - the wall clock had become a blue globed eye: there was another one close by. And the fireplace had turned into a vast mouth that was beaming at us colossally.

"Aaahhh!" it said in a great outgusting of breath like - like the storms of Mars. "That's better. I was having difficulty with that shape - such complexity packed into so small a size."

"It's what I've always said," Jeff piped up: you creep, I thought. "For all of humanity's failings, we are fairly advanced creatures."

"Some of us, Jeff," I spat out, trying to put anger, fear and a message of caution into the tone. Then I looked at that monstrous mouth. It could swallow us both without trying and probably would, I guessed, despite its friendly expression.

"What are you? What is this place? What do you want?"

I squirmed, realising that I sounded like a bad science fiction movie. The mouth and the eyes, however, considered my questions carefully before replying.

"I am R'ork of the Ischnoides race, from the planet Glareosus in the Vulpeculine cluster. I want to find out about Earth: I want to find out about - you."

"Why?" I wondered, indicating at the same time with my eyes to Jeff that he should try to make a run for it. If I could keep this great mouth-in-the-wall talking, and the huge alien eyes focused my way, Jeff could be in with a chance - as soon as he stopped scribbling stupid notes in his book!

"Like most species," R'ork said, "we of the Ischnoides have built up our population over the years to the point where we must seek new territories. Glareosus is now far too small and cramped, and our urge to expand and explore has driven us outwards to all parts of the galaxy. I came here - and fortunately so, as I did not expect such pleasant and inquisitive company!"

R'ork's red lips parted in a smile. Its teeth were white, and sharp, and as big as housebricks.

"So. Your intention is to use Earth for your own purposes to make it a colony."

"Indeed. Intelligence and curiosity! I am well favoured."

I was running out of questions by now - and nerve. Jeff just sat there nodding eagerly like a bookworm at a philosophy lecture, so I reasoned it was down to me to act.

I reckoned that a mouth embedded in plaster could not inflict much damage if I stayed well away from it, so my plan was to make a dive straight for the door - not going near Jeff, who would have to take his chances. They would not be great, I thought, if he continued talking to this alien as though it was a next-door neighbour.

I tensed up ready to move. And the chair clenched around me.

It happened in an instant. In the space of a breath the arms of the chair rippled, suddenly bulging and pulsing with veins: artificial fibre became skin, foam filling became muscles. R'ork's huge impassive eyes swung to glare at me, and the mouth in the wall began to laugh.

That's when I stopped thinking and started acting. I had a metal ballpoint pen in my pocket, and did not hesitate: I held it hard in my fist and jabbed it down into the chair.

R'ork's bellowing laugh lifted upward to a scream of pain. The chair-arm bled, and the whole piece of furniture began thrashing around me. Jeff, who had been watching all of this with mouth open, put up his hands as though to stop traffic.

"Louis. No - this isn't the way. We must compromise with these creatures. Reason with them."

"Stuff your compromise!" I yelled. "I'm being eaten by an armchair, and you want to reason with it! Just get yourself moving!"

The muscular feel of the thing around me abated, became jellylike and amorphous. I pushed myself away from it and ran.

I leaped headfirst through the doorway as the door began to swing shut. While it did, it was transforming into a lobe of flesh that reached itself towards me.

"Jeff! Get out!"

Jeff of course stood there like a nail, torn between saving himself and establishing détente with an alien blob from the Vulpeculine cluster. He and I glanced up together as the ceiling sagged and became a searching tongue.

I cried out in terror, and left my friend behind. R'ork had not stopped his screaming during this, but now it was more like a roar; angry, predatory.

A bubble swelled in the wall beside me. It expanded to a face - a white and featureless thing, just enough of a face to be able to see and speak to me.

"Face facts," R'ork said, in a gentle voice now, punctuating the barrage of sound that the house was making. "You cannot win, because you cannot predict my actions. What do you know of me? What will I do next?"

"You murderer. You killed Jeff!"

"How do you know that?" R'ork began, but I was already swinging my fist.

The face opened into a tunnel lined with teeth, and I just managed to divert my blow as the tunnel clamped closed with an adder's hiss.

Now I was almost out of the place, which was beginning to drop the facade of being a house: banisters became bones, plaster lost its smoothness and sharp edges, windows membraned over and grew opaque.

"Come on," said the letter box, "let's sit and talk about this."

A chair surged into being from the soft toffee of the floor. It was a gesture of a chair, more like a cupped hand held out.

I jumped round it, pulled aside the floppy front door and belted down the driveway.

The cold air of evening made me gasp more than my mad dash for the road. Once I looked back as I sat astride the barred gate.

The house that was R'ork - illuminated internally somehow - towered and sang around the ruined shell of what must have been Glebe House, probably the template for R'ork's first camouflage on this Earth.

It led me to wonder if maybe the creature could not move easily, in which case it would still be there when the police arrived: police, army, marines, any damn body I could get out here!

I hurried to the telephone kiosk, keeping a wary eye open for R'ork or any of its manifestations. I had no money, but an emergency call would be free.

I picked up the receiver. No dialing tone. Only R'ork's voice.

"Hello Louis. I told you that you couldn't win. Meet my son."

In my hand the telephone writhed into something red and grinning. The glass of the booth thickened over. And suddenly I couldn't find the door.

※　　※　　※　　※　　※

The Forever Man

Everybody knows that empty old houses are haunted, and the one in Patchley Woods was no different. It was a lost house in a forgotten wood. Well, forgotten except by the town kids who sometimes went up there, mainly in the summer: there was no-one around at autumntime, except me, Daz and Simon - and they'll all tell you at the High School that we're crazy.

The fact is, I like spooky places, windblown nowheres full of cold wind and loneliness. Sounds odd, eh? Point is, people get on my nerves. They love themselves, love talking about what they do right, love grumbling about everyone else. It's so boring, you wouldn't believe. They're all like that at Kenniston, living in small circles, making no mark on life. Maybe it's the same in your town?

I know, what's so great about me? Nothing, and I don't pretend there is. I just keep out of the way and dream my dreams, and wonder about the things that most people never worry over - like why Patchley Woods is so deserted, and why the old Lodge stands there in the middle of it with no path leading to the front door and none going out from the back. Maybe the fact that it would cost a fortune to renovate the place has something to do with it. And who'd bother anyway? With the new bypass around the town, no-one travels through Kenniston any more. Truck-drivers hauling freight from the east coast ports to the Midlands thunder by without glancing at the signs: reps head for the bigger towns with a bit of life: tourists go north to the Peaks or south and west to the Cotswolds.

Kenniston, deep green backwater in a busy stream, with everyone living in little circles. Me, a bit bored, a bit angry, trying to hope that life is bigger than the way I see it.

Oh yes, and Daz and Simon.

Well, Daz - Darren Phipps - is a boff. You know what I mean, a real big-brain. Kids hate him because he's clever and he will Go Far. All the teachers tell him that. Oxford, Cambridge. They've practically awarded him the degree already. But he's not, like, God's gift to girls: ears like radar dishes, freckles that almost join up to make one huge freckle on his plain-featured face, and these thick-lensed glasses that give him a real mad-professor-on-some-other-planet look. Whoever marries Daz will do it for blind love, unless of course he makes his fortune, which he's quite likely to before he's twenty-one. He's the sort of kid who'll invent a starship engine the size of a walnut, or something not quite so banal.

Then there's Simon Greaves. Not a lot to say about him. He's a shadow in everybody's sunshine, a thin grey kid from the children's home up Granville Street. Sim looks as though everything's been drained out of him by life. Kids keep telling him he belongs in a Dickens novel, and they're being complimentary. He cries if he gets cold in winter, and he has about as much strength in his bones as an over-boiled cabbage. Simon is as lonely and empty as the places I like to visit, so he tags along with us two because we tolerate him. He's the closest thing to a ghost without being dead that I can imagine.

It's an odd partnership, the three of us alone together. I suppose the truth is we don't make one complete person between us. All weird in our own ways. It's how I want it.

I'll tell you about the woods. First thing to know, there's acres of them. I mean, you could get lost there all day and eventually find your way out late at night with the moon up, almost without realising the day was over. It's happened. I don't know who owns all that land, and I don't know anyone who does know. The person who owns the Lodge I guess, but that house has been empty longer than I've been around. I even checked up in the town library once, because the man who built the house must have been important to Kenniston once; wealthy, influential, a merchant or a banker or something. But there was no record. The librarian didn't even know such a place existed, and threw me out when I argued and started giving her some lip.

The house lies at the centre of the wood, I've decided, at its heart; protected by it, hidden by it. Great stretches of beech and some oak fill the head of the valley between the two arterial roads that strike out north-west and north-east from Kenniston. And somewhere in there lies the Lodge. Can't tell you exactly where, there's no path. But it's there. All private ground of course, signs and rusted barbed wire everywhere. But who takes any notice of them? Besides, three kids wandering don't hurt anybody. Wandering keeps us out of trouble round the estates.

After the long summer holiday came the long autumn term. By October the gold had spilled its way through Patchley and tarnished all of the hillsides. There was a nip in the air by late afternoon, and evening followed quickly. The stars were out by eight.

Daz and Simon still came with me to the woods: along the torn-up railway line and then down the footpath that parallels the boundary of the Lodge estate.

We went there a couple of times a week, when homework was light or there was nothing on the telly. Usually I'd phone Daz and we'd haggle over a time to meet: me, I was ready to go at once, but that kid always had piles of reading to do, stuff about space or fossils or technology. I swear he'll need to stick a hard drive in his ear one of these days to hold on to all the facts.

Then one of us would ring the children's home and tell the warden that we'd call round for Simon. The bloke didn't seem to mind, saying he was glad the boy was making some proper friends at last. We'd always delivered him back on time before, and in one piece. Anyway, who really would have been heartbroken if he'd never come back at all one night? Some people have no real soulmates: some, like Simon, are slightly luckier and can count on one or two. But these folk are half-faded out of existence in the first place, just a smudge on the world. They don't seem fully part of things. Simon was one of them. Always was. Always will be.

It was getting on for the third week in October, I remember, and the prospect of half-term was now more than just a distant mark on everyone's calendar. Along with that time of year came Hallowe'en, Guy Fawkes', then the darkening tunnel of days towards Christmastime.

There was a lot to get excited about, but the three of us still did not care to break our routine. On the Tuesday I arranged with Daz to go for a walk up to the woods, and we passed a message to Simon in Maths which, luckily, was not intercepted by Six Pack (Mr Paulson our pot-bellied Maths teacher). Otherwise we'd have landed in detention.

So, it was organised. At home I stuffed down a quick tea, scribbled out my English essay - A Perfect Summer Holiday (demonstrating your understanding of the difference between a hyphen and a dash) - and walked round to Daz's place in time for the six o'clock deadline. It was uptown, where the BMWs sleep cosily in their integral double garages and daddy rakes the leaves off the swimming pool each weekend. Amazing really, that half a mile away Simon was waiting for us in his jumblesale jacket, not knowing where his father was now, not really caring whether he went back to his home tonight or never.

"You're in a rush," Daz said, matching my fast cruising pace through town with a ridiculous jogtrot of his own

"I want to get there while it's still light. There'll be plenty of time for your stargazing later."

Daz had brought his binocs, pair of Zeiss 7x50s, the best for the job.

"By half-nine Aldebaran will be well up," he told me happily, "and the Pleiades. But I really want to catch Jupiter if I can."

"Catch Jupiter…"

"What?"

"Nothing," I said, irritated and not knowing why. "Let's get a move on."

We picked Simon up and made for Patchley. He trotted behind like a mongrel stray, not going anywhere special, but perfectly happy to be with us.

Daz demanded a rest halfway there. We'd climbed a bit and left the town behind and below us. It was a dark bed of streetlights with a few landmarks recognisable, especially the church floodlit near the town square. The woods formed a darker smear across the skyline ahead of us, and above them the sky glowed blue and violet, and a single star shimmered as though it would shatter.

"It's Capella," Daz confirmed for us. "Fourth brightest star in the whole sky."

"Great," I said. Daz shook his head and smiled his mad-professor smile and gazed at us in some amazement.

"Doesn't it interest you?"

"Knowing its name doesn't much. But the fact that it's there is pretty cool."

"I sometimes wonder what's out there," he said, kind of quietly and intimately as though he were confessing a sin. "You know, whether there are people like us – or not like us!" He giggled. "And if we'll meet them one day… These seem to me to be really important ideas. Really important."

I nodded and glanced briefly at Simon, who was still trying to puzzle out the human beings he'd met in his life. But there was no point trying to out-logic Daz. His teachers said he had his head in the clouds, but I knew his heart was somewhere beyond them.

We stared at the star a while longer. It looked like the broken fragment of a prism; the fourth brighest star in the sky - and then moved on.

The atmosphere changes as soon as you walk into a wood. Even this late in the year, when trees are starting to lose their leaves, enough of a canopy remains to keep the air just pleasantly cool and still, and shut out the noise of the world.

We used our regular gap in the barbed wire fencing, squirming through a screen of hawthorn bushes whose crimson fruits stood out brightly in the gloom. The soil was loamy, moist and scented - but messy. I slipped almost at once and put my right knee to the ground. I could feel the wet seep through instantly, and these were my second best jeans.

"Oh, damn it!"

Simon giggled behind me. It'll be your turn soon enough, I thought maliciously.

We spent twenty minutes wandering. I love to soak up the atmosphere. Daz did his usual and picked up acorns and leaves and other bits of stuff for 'specimens'.

"You must have piles of this junk at home." He nodded.

"Hey, shovel in the leaves through the window, shovel out the compost through the door!"

"Very funny Rob," Daz said. It was too dark to see if he was smiling.

"You got a torch?" I asked. I knew Daz had, in his collecting bag. I heard him rummaging and then the light dazzled us all - "Turn it out!"

"God Almighty Rob," Daz said in a whisper, "I swear I haven't turned it on!"

Even as he said it, I realised that it was true. This was not torchlight, but a huge flood of brilliance washing through the wood. The light was everywhere, making the shadows of the trees look as black and solid as the trunks and branches themselves.

"Close encounters," Simon said pointlessly, making a little gasping sound as the shock sank in.

We dropped down into an undergrowth of ferns, just in case Simon's comment had substance, and crouched there very still, very quiet.

"It's coming from the house," Daz murmured after a moment.

"But there's no electricity at the house..."

And Daz looked at me as if to say, don't be so naive.

The beam - or whatever it was - held steady for maybe three minutes; a soundless, intense bluish light that must have had megawatts of power behind it.

Then it blinked out, instantly, and again without a sound. Simon gave a cry of surprise and we were all left with green after-images of trees standing in a purple night.

"Stay still," I warned, feeling dizzy and disoriented. "Don't run yet."

I wondered why I felt like panicking. We'd not been hurt or even threatened, and we'd not seen anything except that incredible brilliance. Electricity Board, secret military testing station, hallucination, starship from far flung corners of the sky, something worse?

It might be anything, I told myself, then checked that: no, it was nothing normal. I knew why I wanted to run.

There came a sound, again from the direction of where we thought the house would be. This time it was identifiable, the crush-crush of someone coming through bracken, the thumping of heavy footsteps on packed earth. But the pattern of the steps was odd, more like a horse's brisk cantering than a man moving along.

"Let's get out of it," Daz urged, the words whispered and trembling in my ear. "I don't want to know what that is…"

"Not even the name of it?" I snapped back pettily, but I knew how his stomach must be churning. The urge to bolt was strong, but squatting here quietly was the only control we had over the situation. Once we broke cover and legged it for the fence we'd have no more choice in the matter, and our presence would be known.

So we waited. I had my hand clamped to Daz's shoulder - to stop him darting like a rabbit: Simon leaned across and grabbed hold of my jacket hem. We felt safer for each other.

The sound of movement never vanished entirely. It ebbed and flowed through the woods as though whoever was making it didn't know the way out. Sometimes the clumping faded almost away, but then would come a heavy crash, branches lashing this way and that, the snap of wood, then the drumming again as the horse searched for a different route to freedom.

That was it of course! I almost slumped with relief. A horse from one of the local hunt stables must have broken loose and come blundering through Patchley in a panic: the lights were most likely from a Land Rover: men must be all around us trying to catch the animal, trying to stop it bolting and hurting itself -

There were lights again, not the single blistering blaze of a searchlight, but coloured sparkles spiralling deep through the trees. Odd… Car tail-lights maybe? A fire?

The reds and yellows seemed to gather themselves, then come hurtling between the trees with a fierce crackling that rasped and snapped in the air.

Against the whirlpool of sparks was outlined the shape of a man on a horse, riding dextrously, trying to keep to the shadows. But the shower of lights sped closer, moving now towards us.

"Where," Daz asked me, "is the horse's head?"

I nearly turned round and belted him, but what he said was true. I could see it now. There was no man, no horse, but a something that was both. A creature that didn't exist was galloping closer, trying to dodge a supernatural fire.

Daz strained to pull away. The man-horse grunted, leaped across a toppled bough and thundered past, speckling us with flecks of dirt and bits of stick. With a whoosh like a skyrocket the ball of sparks followed him, missed him and burst against a tree. For an instant the oak was made of gold thread and Christmas lights, sparkling like lacework. Then the darkness came and the soundlessness of night, and the air was charged with a dry metallic tingle of energy.

Now we stood awkwardly. We had stiffened into our crouch and it was painful to rise, like coming out of a shared impossible nightmare.

"Home James," I muttered, my voice cracked and croaking, the attempt at humour hopelessly failing.

We knew that the woods were not empty. What we had just seen looked like a chase, and the man-horse thing had escaped.

"It was a centaur," Daz said, following my line of thought. He came out with it as casually as you please. Stupid to argue with him. I knew what it was.

"Odd though – " Daz was babbling to himself. "Centaurs were supposed to be wise, kind, patient. They taught the Greek heroes to ride and shoot with a bow."

111

"Maybe this one didn't get paid…"

Now we were quite close to the hedge, the fence, the open fields and the way home.

"Where's the gap?" Simon wondered. We dared not switch on the torch to look, but strained to see without it instead.

"About – there."

But someone was blocking the way. A man this time, an ordinary man, around my height: a bit scruffy looking, in a tatty green cord jacket, black trousers and muddy brown boots. There were twigs in his fairish hair, and he was holding one arm as though it pained him.

It jolted me to realise that we could see him: everything else was smothered out by darkness. And he could see us too, plainly.

"You boys. This is private ground."

"Yeah, we're just on our way out of it."

I thought the slightly laid-back, not-quite-insolent approach would work best, show him we weren't really scared, even though I wanted to pee myself desperately. Teachers normally responded to this one. But the man just stood there. Maybe he shook his head. I couldn't see him smiling.

He walked over to us and I gasped. He was just a man, not sinister looking or anything, and he was in a sorry state; face smeared with blood, skin pale and stretched, his dusty clothes torn and frayed…

But he had the look of a king, and his eyes were as young as the stars.

"You saw it, didn't you? Everything that happened."

He was not asking us. It was as though our minds were glass to him. He just knew.

"We saw it," Daz admitted, probably wisely. If this character was mixed up in what we'd seen, there was no telling what he could do, though I saw no malice in his face. Perhaps I saw a little pleading.

"It is not safe to leave these woods yet. The creature you saw is still here, also searching for an exit."

"Can't he jump the fence?" The thought of a centaur trotting down Kenniston High Street suddenly made me want to giggle.

"The fences guarding this wood are not made entirely of barbed wire." He said this with a wry smile, gone again in a flash. "My defences are not perfect."

"Your defences?" Darren said. "You own Patchley, and the Lodge?"

"As far as it can be owned, I own it. I, er, I manage the estate." Once more the tired remnants of what had been a sharp wit and a bright sense of humour surfaced and sank. I felt that this man was not dangerous to us, and that he needed help. He breathed out truth. Already he was a friend.

"Can't we go home then?" Simon asked innocently.

"Not yet."

And Simon smiled, like this was some kind of chance he had been waiting for. I pushed it further.

"But we can't stay out here, with that thing roaming around and you injured."

"I know. We must go to the house."

No-one argued, me least of all. The prospect of following the field path back to town while knowing what was out prowling was not a pleasant one. Besides, in a strange way I was hooked by curiosity. Here was somebody who talked about centaurs as if they were an everyday sight. What else had he seen? And who was he? And why did he live in a derelict house in the middle of nowhere? Material for my next English essay, I thought wryly: but classrooms and homework seemed a million miles away right now.

Of course, the house was not derelict, not with the man there to brush away the cobwebs of the illusion. True enough, the outer walls were crumbling and the windows were glassless black holes, and the smell of mould and rotting wood was rich in the air. But once inside things were different.

We went down a long passageway. At first cracked stone tiles gritted under our shoes, and our footsteps echoed from damp walls, But as we went further the air turned warm, the walls grew smooth and new: around us like a transformation the house became well-maintained and lived in, this man's home.

For all that, the place was big and rambling. Some of the corridors were dark and obviously rarely visited, and curiously lit with a mixture of softly hissing gas brackets and modern electric lamps.

Finally we came to a big pine door, the bare wood glowing with a rich varnish.

The man pushed it open and led us through into a study.

I smelled books and old leather, sweet tobacco smoke and plastic: and again, that prickly electrical smell in the air that I'd first noticed in the woods.

"It's a beautiful place," Daz said, staring around as we all did. Bookshelves lined two walls and went right up to the ceiling. A third wall was taken up with metal racks of files, tapes, discs - and a stack of machines that was like a cross between the world's most sophisticated hi-fi and Mission Control at Houston.

Finally there was the man's desk, facing the window; a huge bay window with heavy green curtains pulled across.

"Amazing," Simon added. And I had to admit that I was impressed too.

Out of the dark, we became aware of the state we were in. My muddy knee seemed a bit pathetic, as we were all spotted with mud, our clothes soiled, jumpers snagged, hair wet, faces smeared. And the arm of the man's jacket was soaked in fresh blood.

"That looks pretty bad," Daz said, instantly concerned.

"Shall we ring for a doctor?"

The man looked at me levelly. "That would not be a wise move. He would have difficulty finding a way through the woods, and what roams there might yet find an escape."

I shrugged. "We'd better do something ourselves then. Got any bandages?" I tried to sound casual but my stomach was rolling.

After a moment he nodded towards a table that was littered with bits of apparatus, a microscope, books scattered and open, and an ornamental box. Daz went over, opened it and took out bandage and antiseptic, while Simon helped the man off with his jacket and shirt.

The wound was deep and still bleeding. It was not a knifecut, but whatever caused it had been sharp, heavy and expertly used.

"The hooves of centaurs are not to be taken lightly." He smiled a pale smile of pain. He knew as well as we did that bandages were not going to be of any use whatsoever.

"Which brings me," I said - loudly, to conceal the fact that I wanted to throw up, "to the sixty-four thousand dollar question. What are centaurs doing in Patchley Woods?"

Daz poured on neat antiseptic, then proceeded to make a botchjob of bandaging. But at least the wads of cotton staunched the blood and seemed to make the man more comfortable.

He went and sat down in one of his study chairs, his jacket draped around him. The room was warm enough, though I could see no sign of heating. We sat close by, Daz and Simon on the floor, while I pulled up his desk chair. It was like story time at school, only on this occasion I knew that we weren't going to be told make-believe. This was happening to us, and it was going to be true.

"Imagine a frontier bordering many lands. There are various reasons why people remain in their own countries: reasons why some try to cross from one nation to another. Whether this is desirable or not, such frontier-posts must be guarded, and vulnerable peace-loving races protected from those that are strong and warlike.

"But I want you to think of worlds rather than lands, of other places and times that in part do not even exist in this universe. These too have their borderlands, their frontiers: and these too have their refugees and their invading armies. Crossing points must be guarded, boundaries monitored and patrolled – "

"But who trespasses in Patchley Woods, except for kids?" Daz wanted to know. Either he was being abnormally thick, or sarcastic. And for once I really didn't know which.

I began to wonder. Maybe it was a man on a horse that we'd seen, perhaps the authorities had been out - perhaps tracking down a madman who told stories of other universes. The idea made me feel cold.

The man eased himself stiffly out of his chair and walked to the window. He took the curtain-pull and stared straight at us.

"You are still not sure of me, I see that; not understanding that I don't talk of trees and fields, but of stars."

He drew open the curtains, then went over and switched out the lights.

The night outside was windblown and dark. And someone had lit a fire, for white sparks glittered through the trees and...

My perspective tilted sideways and spun round. I almost toppled forward, off balance and dizzied to realise that these were not sparks, but stars as the man had said, clouds of them, drifts of stars piled high against black nothingness. And the glow, that red bonfire glow, was a much larger star, a sun nothing like our own sun: it turned slowly and hugely into view, a faint cloud of shining gas like rosy veils of fog.

Then the vision was gone. The lights blazed back and washed out the sight - but not the memory of it, ever.

Three of us stood there dumbstruck. Tears were dropping from Daz's eyes, but not unhappy tears: and Simon looked as serious as I had ever seen him.

"So," the man said softly, "now you know for sure. You are the only ones on this world ever to know, though others have suspected, for occasionally a creature breaks through from another place and in time contributes to the folklore and legends of history.

"A thousand or two thousand years ago I could afford to let them free. They were the persecuted of their own domains, the outcasts. They did no damage here and often greatly enriched Earth's cultures. But some came to destroy or conquer, and these I must send back. Besides, times have changed. People have changed. The human mind is no longer open enough to treat the outsiders as your ancestors did."

"And the centaur is still on the loose!" Simon reminded us. The man nodded.

"Still free, still dangerous. And it is also true that the barriers surrounding this wood have been breached: I thank you for discovering the break by your entry, but that entry must be sealed. It could also make an exit."

"We'll help you," Daz said eagerly. "Four of us could easily catch the thing. And, well, I don't know about the others, but this is just about the best time I've ever had!"

"These are not games and childish adventures." The man led us towards the door. "I am grateful, but my concern is to see you safely on your way. There is much work for me to do, and the places I guard are not playgrounds. Go now: you may not be so easily spotted in the dark."

We went out into the night, the real October night with its high gusting winds that made the trees boom, and fast fleeting clouds underlit orange by the streetlamps of the town: following the man, not arguing, but heavy with the knowledge of what we had seen and the fact that we would never see it again.

"Careful now," he said at one point. "I sense that the creature is near."

I felt exposed and frightened at the end of the line. Ahead of me, Daz trotted on like a little dog, while Simon held the man's coat-hem tightly, like a son would stay close to his father.

I shivered, not just because of the cutting wind, and listened hard through the crash of branches and whoosh of thrashed leaves.

The sound ebbed and flowed hugely, ebbed and flowed as the big autumn wind came rushing over the Midland plain, swept across the town and up the valley.

Then out of that sound rose the sharper noise of undergrowth crackling. A big, heavy creature snorted nearby - frighteningly close - and thudded out of darkness and tree cover from the left, plunging straight for us.

It was the centaur, could be nothing else, and its eyes winked like two gold coins spun in the air. We began to turn, reacting to its approach. Daz started to call out a late and pointless warning.

The man-animal reared up, chopping with its deadly fore hooves. I saw the arch of a strong proud neck and the glint of light on its white teeth: then I ducked as a hoof went cleaving overhead, churning into bushes and bracken a mere foot away.

The thing's powerful body spun and battered me over, smashing me down. Daz too was on his back, Simon a short way off and diving for safety.

The centaur reared, breath whistling, shouting in a language that seemed neither music nor speech. But the threat was there, the clear intention to kill us.

I rolled frantically, felt the thump-slap of the hoof driving into earth where my head had just lain. The blow would have crushed my skull like a thin shell.

I tried to roll further, out of harm's way, and came up against a barbed screen of brambles. My jacket sleeve was caught, thorns already scratching through to my skin as I struggled.

And now the centaur reared again, towering, sure of the kill. I threw up my hand, knowing that it would be like trying to stop a train.

The night erupted silently, scalding away the dark in the blaze of white light that we had seen before. The creature flinched from it, the centaur's man-face showing anger and fear, its eyes flashing red as fire.

"Scramble clear!" the man's voice called out. I wriggled free of my jacket and dived, twisting round in time to see the light disintegrate into showering glimmers and sparks that ran along the outline of the centaur's body.

Then the sparks thinned, and as they did so the outline became vaguer, less clearly defined, until I could not distinguish it from the night itself. The high shrill cut glass cry of the centaur's defeat blended with the wind in the leaves and its presence with the cold loneliness of the woods.

I started to tremble, realising how close I'd been to dying. Daz nearby was wiping his face, trying not to show his little boy's perfectly reasonable terror.

"You OK Simon?" I asked.

Simon was standing beside the man, opening the front of his green cord jacket.

"Bleeding's started again. I'll help you back to the house."

I expected the man to argue, but he didn't. After a moment's thought and silence, he handed Simon a small torchlike device - probably the thing he'd used to send the centaur back to its domain. And it seemed like more than just a casual gesture of trust, an accepted offer of assistance.

"Hey, Simon," I said, not quite understanding why, "we'll wait for you down by the fence, right?"

The two of them walked off through the trees into darkness. We turned and went the other way.

At the boundary I scrambled through first, then held the wire for Daz to follow. I started off down the hill, hands jammed into pockets, shrugging out the chill.

"We said we'd wait," Daz reminded me. I turned, looked back up at him.

"Yeah, I'm sure. I just feel sorry I never said a proper goodbye, that's all."

There were questions, many questions; and suspicion and then a kind of resignation. Maybe the man's influence was in it somewhere, but no full-scale police searches followed, and after six months Simon's name was never mentioned except between Darren and me.

Now I can barely remember what he looked like.

We still go up to Patchley, just the two of us, and wander about through the beeches and the oaks. We've never seen the blinding light again or heard the night-time wails of things that were not foxes or owls. And we've never again found the place where that old house had stood, at the crossroads where we all choose our way.

*   *   *   *   *

Burning

They told me that I would never leave here, and I believe them, for I have tested that truth.

At first, when I was very young and they brought me to Genco, I thought it was a school. There were lots of other children here, and we played and we learned. My parents were upset to let me go, but they had been instructed to do it by the Dominus, and were honoured to obey even though their hearts were broken. They said that they would come to see me as often as they could, but Deevis who leads us said that would not be possible. They wondered why, I remember: and I wondered why. But now I know.

I remember, too, my first talk with Deevis. In those days, in the early time, he was gentle and kind, but still there was a little fear in his eyes. We walked away from the Complex into the grounds where the birds sang and the trees whispered. We sat in an open space that was bright and warm with sunlight, and Deevis gave me some chocolate.

"Brin," he said, "I want to answer some of your questions. That is necessary if you are to enjoy a happy life here at Genco."

He paused for a moment and looked at the sky, as though reflecting. Then he looked at me with eyes that held hope and curiosity and many other things. He smiled.

"You are a very special boy, you know. In the same way, all of the children who come to us are special. The Dominus knows of your existence. He calls you The Favoured Ones."

"Bless and keep the Dominus," I said, without really thinking: it was what I was meant to say.

"Bless and keep him," Deevis echoed, and smiled in a way that I could not quite understand.

"You know, of course, that you are studying with us and not at a normal school because you are not like most other children."

I nodded. He went on softly:

"Here you will be trained both to control and to use your powers in the service of the Dominus. Tell me, what do you understand your powers to be?"

I thought about that hard, because I had never put it into words before. What I did had always been a feeling. I said, "I can make the trees shed their leaves. I can make people grow old. I can make the sun and moon spin like coins in the sky."

It made me chuckle, because that was funny to see. But Deevis stared at me as though he was greatly disturbed.

"That is an interesting way to put it, Brin. And indeed, that is how you see it happening. Scientifically, we say that you have the power to pass through time - STT, Spontaneous Temporal Translocation. When people grow older, it is because you have jumped into their futures, years ahead to them, but an instant in time to you. Do you understand?"

"Yes sir," I answered, but I was not sure that I did.

"Good. And there is one other piece of information that you must also understand and remember. Otherwise life for you and for us at Genco could be very dangerous."

Deevis tried to speak in a friendly way, but I saw the corners of his mouth twitching, just a tiny bit.

"Strictly speaking it is not true to say that you pass through time, Brin: rather, time passes through you. You are like a lens that focuses the energy we call chronotrons - minutes and seconds, days and months and years. Now, what happens if you focus sunlight on paper?"

"It burns," I said. That was easy. "The paper burns away to nothing."

"Yes, that's right. It burns. Listen to me now; although we may want you to move into the future - to make the trees shed their leaves - you must never open yourself to it completely. You must never jump as far as you can, because the whole energy of your life would be focused into the millionth part of an instant. Do you understand me, Brin?"

This time I could not nod. Deevis said: "Never ever make the moon spin too fast, Brin. Yes?"

I can't remember now if I answered him, because it interested me so much to see him trembling.

*   *   *   *   *

Over the years I learned many lessons and saw many strange sights. At Genco the techniks taught me to use my power sparingly, so that I thought of seconds like grains of gold that were not to be squandered. Once, when I was late back to my room after talking to Karel, my truest friend, I jumped-on to morning so that the doors would be unlocked. Deevis was there waiting with two men from Security. They were frightened, all of them, but Deevis was angry too. It was the first and only time he ever hit me for what I had done. Both of us knew then that he would never dare to try it again.

I told Karel about it later and she sympathised. I think, out of all the people I knew, she was the kindest, and she alone did not look on me with fear.

Her gift, she told me, was to see into people. Not really into their bodies, but in a thought-feel way into their heads and their hearts. I suppose she saw something of what would become of them.

"And what will become of me, Karel?" I wondered. The day was bright and scented outside the Genco Complex. I think people called it May.

Karel stared at the sky. "There will be many days like this, Brin. But dark days too. Days of war, I think…"

"Like what - days like what?"

"With me beside you, loving you Brin."

Karel leaned close and kissed me. Her blonde hair crossed my eyes and made the sun shimmer. I lay with her and I thought, as it was happening, that Burning must be like this.

This is how it would be to make the sun twirl like a coin.

Some time later Deevis talked to us about the War. He spoke to all of us together, as well as seeing each of us alone. As his voice boomed in the auditorium I watched the faces of the others. Some of them did not look quite like people, but each of their expressions was the same.

"So," Deevis said in finishing, "we must all play a part in helping the Dominus to fight the threat of the Merikan-Sovyet advance. Our future lies in saving the futures of everyone. God bless and keep the Dominus."

"Bless and keep him," I whispered with the rest, and wondered where Merikan-Sovyet might be in the world.

In the months that followed, many of the Genco children left to fight in the War. They were really young men and young women, although in what they said, and in the way that pride and terror were mixed in their eyes, they still seemed like children. One of them, a geopath called Sonda, said he was part of a Genetically Controlled Counter-Terrorist Force. Deevis had told him, Sonda said. But when I asked what the words meant, Sonda didn't know and we both laughed about it. He waved back at me from the front gate, and that was the last I saw of him ever.

Winter came and life grew dull. I wanted so much to jump-on to the warmer days of summer, but I realised that would mean leaving Karel behind: that is, the Karel of this moment. If I did it, she would be six months older and I would not have aged at all. I knew too, that if I started to ignore my lessons and drift futurewards out of curiosity or selfishness, then I would not be able to stop. Compulsion to see how the world went would draw me on through eternity. And, as Deevis had warned, that could be dangerous: to look upon forever would mean the Burning.

But I was bored. I saw Deevis about it. "I don't understand," I told him, "why you don't send me to the War. Am I not fit and strong like - like Sonda for instance?"

"You are fit and strong, Brin," Deevis said, "and the Dominus would be pleased with your loyalty. As for Sonda, he was useful as a weapon to be dispatched and, if necessary, sacrificed. But you are too valuable to be sent away."

"Why?" I wondered. Deevis considered his answer carefully.

"Because the world has never seen a power like yours. We are not sure exactly what it is, or what it might develop into. Only future generations of temperopaths will solve that puzzle."

"Future generations?" That confused me, because my parents were not Favoured, and I had no brothers or sisters who might want –

Then Deevis told me about Karel and our child, and that although this was our purpose in the eyes of the Domirinus, Karel truly loved me and wanted our baby to live and be brought up at Genco.

I asked if I might see Karel: she had not been allowed out of her rooms for weeks, but Deevis shook his head.

"She is resting, Brin, and under the care of many doctors."

I held Deevis's arm gently.

"I am going to see her, Deevis," I said, only quietly, and he did not have the power to stand in my way.

Karel looked beautiful in her bed, despite the automedic machines that glinted and moved around her. Her eyes lit as she saw me, but then grew dark and moist. She began to cry.

"You know," she said, "that they have done this to us? The whole reason for us being here was to produce what is inside me now."

I nodded, yet only realising it as she spoke.

Karel went on. "I don't think they are really interested in me - maybe in you Brin, because of your gift. They want our child! They want to see what she is and what she can do. They are going to use her, Brin, to help win their filthy War!"

Karel's hands were shaking in anger. Red monitor lights came up on a wallscreen.

"'She'," I whispered. "You can see that?"

"I feel it," Karel said. "I see that the future glows with light."

Tears dropped from her eyes, and she covered them with her quivering hands. "The future is so bright, Brin. So bright..."

I think I had never felt so sick and betrayed as I did then. I felt hot rage building up in my chest. It came to me that for all these years I had believed the word of the Dominus - God bless and keep him, a mind-voice sang - but that perhaps he was wrong, and that the Merikan-Sovyet was fighting for what was right. And good.

I sat beside Karel on the bed and held her. Alarms chattered nearby and shrieked in the corridors. The arms of the machines quickly withdrew.

"We can stop what we fear," I said gently, not frightened now, because she was with me. "Our daughter does not have to be a weapon for the Dominus, or an experiment for Deevis to watch. We do not have to be prisoners here any longer."

I sounded strong, but I knew I could do it only if Karel was with me.

I heard footsteps hammering closer, and men were shouting.

"They want to kill you Brin."

Karel turned her head to look at me and she smiled, and she nodded.

The door banged open and Deevis was there with Security men behind him. They were armoured like grey tanks, and their guns were pointed at my head.

Deevis held them back, then opened his hands to me.

"Please, Brin. Can't you see what it means - a human being who can see the future and go there to use it, to bend it to our will!"

"You know nothing of human beings, Deevis," I said very softly. "And now I am going to make the moon spin."

Deevis yelled, "Kill him!"

But it was too late. I held Karel close and opened my heart. And eternity burst around me like the sun.

*　　*　　*　　*　　*

About the Author

I was born and raised in the mining valleys of South Wales. My favourite place to play was out on the hills where my imagination had plenty of space to expand.

When I was ten I joined the Double Dare Gang. We used to dare each other to do things, but the one who made up the dare got *double* dared - so he had to do it too. If you didn't do the dare you were a yellow-belly chicken, and if it happened more than three times you were thrown out of the gang.

My family moved up to the Midlands when I was thirteen. At my new school I was put into a French class but didn't know any French. So the teacher Miss Molloy (Mollie) made me sit in the naughty corner 'And get on with something constructive.'

That's when I started to write, just for myself. And I've been doing it ever since.

I have always loved BIG IDEAS and strange places, which is why I write a lot of Science Fiction, Fantasy and Horror. I think that well told stories of this sort are like the fairy tales of old. They teach you important things to help you along in the world.

I'm twelve years old on the inside, older on the outside, and I live in the country with my wife and lots of animals. I like drinking beer, reading, and watching old SF movies on TV.

My aim is not to make a living, but a life.

I'm pretty happy really.

Steve Bowkett

Author Visits

- **Availability:** Any time if given sufficient notice.

- **Sessions:** 1-hour sessions work best for talks, Q/A, readings; longer (90 minutes-2 hours) if workshops are included.

- **Activities:** Storytelling, talks/discussions on writing, SF/Fantasy/Horror; Question & Answer, book signings, readings, more formal lectures, creative writing workshops on poetry or prose, short, INSET seminars and workshops.

- **Age Range:** 7 upwards, inc. adult.

- **Group Size:** Any number for talks or storytelling: max. class size preferred for workshops if children are to participate and work in groups. If audience is larger, Steve will demonstrate w/s activities for children to try out subsequently.

- **Travelling:** Unless the venue is easily accessible from South Leics., Steve will use the train (standard class), travelling to destinations more than a couple of hours from home on the evening prior to the visit.

- **Accommodation:** Steve much prefers to be hosted by a member of staff at the school or library where he is speaking, but will tolerate Hotel/B&B if the premises are licensed. Food: Will consume virtually anything in quantity, but allergic to shellfish. Lunch: Likes to go off-campus for lunch.

- **Book Sales:** Using a local book seller or national book fair (e.g., Scholastic Book Fairs) is preferable. Sale-or-return deals with publishers may be negotiated. Steve will bring limited quantities of his books to sell if requested.

Activities Offered

Storytelling: 1-hour story telling session based loosely around SF/Fantasy genres and Steve's Double Dare Gang stories; using SF, Fantasy and Horror motifs as his metaphors for real-life themes. Tone, a mixture of the serious and light-hearted, incorporating personal experiences and how these can be woven into fiction.

Workshops: Creative thinking/writing activities offered for all ages including adults; general or based around particular themes, or with a certain age/ability-range of children in mind.

Poetry: 1-hour poetry readings interspersed with anecdotes and personal experiences leading to the creation of the poems. Tone varies between stories, light-hearted, reflective. NOTE: that Steve can offer genre-based poetry (SF/Fantasy orientated, mainstream or both. Please specify).

Talks: 1-hour talks on writing, SF, horror, the world of publishing etc. Including some storytelling/readings where appropriate, usually punctuated by Question/Answer sessions.

Residencies: Steve can offer residencies for more extended work with pupils. These would include storytelling and reading sessions, plus workshop activities, as part of a planned programme where author, teacher and children could follow a piece of writing and/or a theme through to completion.

INSET: Four modules are currently available –

- **Imagine That** – developing creative thinking and writing skills.
- **Self-Intelligence** – developing confidence, self-esteem and interpersonal skills.
- **Relaxation & Learning** – developing relaxation and visualisation skills.
- **The Teller & The Tale** – developing storytelling skills as an educational tool.

Recent Author Related Work

- **1998** - Invited to offer INSET (teacher training) workshops in Creative Thinking, Literacy, Developing Emotional Resourcefulness, and Stress Management [on behalf of Network Educational Press/Centre for the Study of Comprehensive Schools - CSCS].

- Member of the Consultative group for the National Advisory Committee on Creative & Cultural Education - NACCCE (a group set up by David Blunkett to explore ways of developing creativity and thinking skills in schools).

- Local advisory writer for the *Stageworks* team - from pen to performance - a group of writers/producers/directors briefed to develop writing and directing skills on a local basis in the Market Harborough area, a project initiated by the Harborough District Arts Development Officer.

- **1999** - Invitation to develop a companion volume to *Imagine That* by Network Educational Press. The project, called *Self-Intelligence,* will focus on practical ways of developing emotional resourcefulness (confidence, self-assurance, sensitivity) in children. Invited on to NEP's Consultancy Team.

- Writing residency at the International Community School, Addis Ababa.

- Involvement in the Northamptonshire Story Festival incorporating visits to several schools.

- Guest Author at Young Readers UK National Book Festival for Children & Young People.

- Week long writing residency at the Matthew Arnold School, Oxford, for feeder primaries.

- Elected as a committee member of the National Association of Writers' Groups.

- **2000** - Three day residency at Normanton Junior School, Derby, as part of the city's Writers In Schools Initiative.

- Four day residency as part of the *Read On Write Away* project at Glossopdale Community College and Phillip Howard School.

- Involvement in Derbyshire's *Millennium Literature Festival.*

- **Ongoing** - Regular visits to schools to run storytelling sessions and short story and poetry workshops for children from 7+ upwards, and throughout the ability range.

Background:

Steve taught English at secondary level for twenty years and is also a qualified Hypnotherapist. He now spends his time writing, running a busy hypnotherapy practice and developing courses to allow people to boost their creative writing and thinking abilities.

- Member of NAWE (the *National Association for Writers in Education*), an organisation which aims to professionalise the status of writers seeking work in schools.
- Member of the *Society of Authors, Children's Writers & Illustrators Group* (CWIG).
- Committee Member of the *National Association of Writers Groups* (NAWG): East Midlands Co-Ordinator and regional editor of their Journal, The Link.
- Tutor for the *Pearse House Organisation,* which promotes and organises creative writing courses for children throughout the country.
- Tutor for *Creative Arts Courses,* founded by Helen Jagger Wood in Camelford, North Cornwall. Tutor for Vera O'Hagan's *Residential Writing Workshops* based at the Old School House, Haltwhistle. Tutor for *Coastal Courses* (for health, creativity & well-being), founded by Anna Harris of Headlands, North Cornwall.
- Tutor for The Writing School based at Leicester Adult Education College.
- Steve has worked as INSET Trainer for Independent Thinking Ltd/Network Educational Press/The Centre for the Study of Comprehensive Schools (CSCS) - and ongoing on a freelance basis.
- Member of the *Consultative Group for the National Advisory Committee on Creative & Cultural Education* - NACCCE (a group set up by David Blunkett to explore ways of developing creativity and thinking skills in schools).

If you would like a more complete CV and/or references, or would like to see more of Steve's work, visit his website at:-

www.sbowkett.freeserve.co.uk

Photocopy

Publications available from
Crazy Horse Press

no p&p, delivery by return, order form overleaf:

The Adventures of Stringy Simon – Peter Hayden

Book 1: Sampler Edition 7 – 12 yrs   ISBN 1 871870 07 0   £4.99

Book 2: The Willy Enlarging Elixir 9 – 13 yrs   ISBN 1 871870 10 0   £4.99

Book 3: The Sneeze & Other Stories 7 – 12 yrs   ISBN 1 871870 11 9   £4.99

'You are my favourite author and I enjoy your books. They are funny.'

'I really like your books, especially Stringy Simon, it is fantastic.'

'I think your book about Stringy Simon and his willy is great.'

'I have not heard of a children's book writer or adult book writer as good as you.'

(Junior readers – originals available)

The Day Trip – Peter Hayden
'Gripped by the pace and realism of the writing we join the school outing and are bussed, sailed and decanted onto French soil. From now on, in spite of their luckless teachers, the kids are on their own, our lot rather more than the rest. Lost and late, they board the wrong boat home, merge with another school, and end up on the wrong side of the Watford Gap. Ah - but Mike and Lee have declared their love; and what a day they've all had. Hayden's an invigorating new talent to watch.'

(The Guardian)   Teens   ISBN 0 19 271 510 0   **£4.95**

And Smith Must Score... – Peter Hayden
'I recommend it to anyone looking for a good footy read.'   (Nick Hornby)

'A wonderful, charming and witty dose of escapist fiction.'   (Derby Co. F.C. fanzine)

'A football supporter's dream of a book.'   (Middlesbrough F.C. fanzine)

'If you're a footy fan counting down the weeks to the new season, then this is the book for you.'   (Observer)   Adults & teens   ISBN 1 871870 08 9   **£6.99**

The Headmaster's Daughter – Peter Hayden
'I really enjoyed reading it. It was like listening in on girls' cloakroom gossip.'
(Berlie Doherty)

'We didn't think you were the type who knew about the words snogging, getting-off, or swearing. Me and Donna thought you were the innocent type (speaking-wise)... We thoroughly enjoyed reading it (we are being serious).'

'It's the kind of book that you would be sort of drifting with when you start reading it but when you'd finished you'd read it again because you realise how it fits together and appreciate the detail given at the beginning.'   (Teenage readers - originals available)

Older teens   ISBN 1 871870 09 7   **£5.99**

Catch & Other Stories – Steve Bowkett
Tales of horror, fantasy and science fiction. Steve Bowkett has 22 teen horror and fantasy titles to his credit, including the popular Dreamcatcher series. His books have been translated into five languages.

'Stephen Bowkett has a rare flair for creating an atmosphere of fear and horror out of the most prosaic of situations. Edgar Allen Poe would have been proud.'

(Junior Bookshelf)

'Bowkett catches the stuff of adolescence.' (Observer)

9 – 12 yrs   ISBN 1 871870 13 5   **£5.99**

The Poppy Factory Takeover & Other Stories – Peter Hayden
Creative writing in the classroom - observations and stunning examples from three decades of writing with the young.

"There is about the whole book a trustworthiness which carries it all – i.e. I like the sound of this ex-teacher writer, he's got experience worth learning from, and you don't lay the learning on heavy man, only say what you believe passionately. I hope this book gets reviewed at length in the right places."   (David Hart, Birmingham Poet Laureate)

Parents, adults and teens   ISBN 1 871870 12 7   **£6.99**

Against The Odds   ISBN 1 871870 02 X

George's Mechanical Sledge   ISBN 1 871870 03 8

I'm Seeing Stars   ISBN 1 871870 01 1

Man's Best Enemy   ISBN 1 871870 00 3

Four humorous stories written and illustrated by teenagers.

9 - 12 yrs   £5.99 - set of four.

'The Keeper Looks Like Elvis'
[Not really a Crazy Horse production - five football sit-com episodes, each in a staple-bound booklet, featuring a non-league team and their fanzine. Written by Peter Hayden & Robert Pant.]

Adults   £5 set of five.

[Order form overleaf]

Photocopy

ORDER FORM

Photocopy and send to: **Crazy Horse Press,**
116 Bewdley Road, Stourport, Worcs DY13 8XH.
Please send me the following books by return:

.... copies of 'The Adventures of Stringy Simon' @ £4.99   = £ ....

.... copies of 'The Willy Enlarging Elixir' @ £4.99   = £ ....

.... copies of 'The Sneeze & Other Stories' @ £4.99   = £ ....

.... copies of 'The Headmaster's Daughter' @ £5.99   = £ ....

.... copies of 'The Day Trip' @ £4.95   = £ ....

.... copies of 'And Smith Must Score...' @ £6.99   = £ ....

.... copies of 'The Poppy Factory Takeover' @ £6.99   = £ ....

.... copies of 'Catch & Other Stories' @ £5.99   = £ ....

.... sets of 'Against The Odds', &c. @ £5.99   = £ ....

.... sets of 'The Keeper Looks Like Elvis' sit-com @ £5.00   = £ ....

TOTAL [no p&p required]   = £ ....

NAME ....

ADDRESS...

....

....POSTCODE ....

PHONE ....

I enclose a cheque for £..

Signed:..